Tales and Yarns from Leicester's Secret Garden.

Derek Charles Goodwin

Derek Charles Goodwin

Book Cover by Richard Paling

Illustrations by Pammie Raymond, Seema Solanki, E Brammal and Jevgenija Zulfugarova. Photo Mat Fascione

First edition 2024

Hardback: 978-1-7385541-0-2

Paperback: 978-1-7385541-1-9

eBook: 978-1-7385541-2-6

Enquiries: UncleDereksStories@outlook.com

Preface

What you have in your hand is a journey into the history and folklore of our wonderful Leicester, also our beautiful shire. It is a collection of fables, yarns and stories written for your entertainment. There are stories of Black Annis, great whirlwinds, stone circles, ghosts, secret places, and all manner of folklore.

I hope you enjoy the stories of the Leicester giants, the secret leper tunnels around New Parks, the meat-eating blackberries, and the pineapple that cost as much as your house! I also hope you enjoy researching the stories and would love to see your surprised looks when you find out the stories are true (well you can decide if they are true!).

Derek Charles Goodwin

Introduction

As someone who is well known locally as a relentlessly talking old windbag full of nonsense, tales, and yarns, one of those people who tortures his wife and young family members with visits to all manner of local places of historical interest (to me), museums, graveyards, and topical talks, I always mused with the idea of a book of sorts! During the covid pandemic whilst redeployed to the enchanting secret garden project at Leicester Glenfield Hospital I found it full of the most incredibly generous and talented volunteers. Along with them was a vast number of recuperating visitors and their relatives to this magical place; it filled my cup with stories. Stories which have overflowed onto paper, and this is what I present to you in the hope you will dip your cerebral biscuit into it with a mix of joyful wonderment at the city and county of Leicester/shire with all the yarns, fables and piffles therein.

I am fully aware, and so should you be dear reader, that this is a collection of fables and yarns as told orally between strangers in a park, families by firelight and eclectic people casually meeting. There are many truths to be found in them, but also inaccuracies, perhaps mistakes and definitely humongous embellishments on my part. The primary purpose of the collection of works is to entertain, but also to preserve story's and promote our local area, to get people looking for themselves, visiting places and asking questions of our local rich historically bejewelled culture and county. If any of the stories are inaccurate, wrong or even made-up whopping works of personal fiction, I make no apologies to the point where I have asked the printer of the book to make sure the paper is splinter free: so, if the only use you can find for the book is to use it as toilet paper, I won't also be a pain in the posterior.

So, if you ever sat on a bus, park bench or picnic table etc and a weird person in some kind of hat comes and starts talking to you, and before you know it you have returned conversation and told them a little story or such like? I am that one who sits next to people like you, and I have saved those (mostly) local stories for this book. Allow yourself a mental tumble down the rabbit hole where you will learn about things such as donkeys' ears, ginger slaves, weeping trees, and creepy witches, with luck you will be done in time for 6 o'clock tea.

Derek C Goodwin.

(Printed on splinter free, flushable paper, I swear on your life!).

Tales and Yarns from Leicester's Secret Garden.

Derek Charles Goodwin

Derek Charles Goodwin

Contents

1

Black Annis, The Black Witch of The Danes Hills.

In the foreboding depths of Leicester Forest, The Danes Hills, Leicestershire, lay an ancient and decaying leper colony, forgotten by the world and ruled by a chilling figure, a medieval nun known as Sister Annis Bower. The once tranquil woods echoed with the moans of the afflicted, their pitiful cries haunting into the souls of those who dared to venture nearby. Even by 1534 when Sister Annis first arrived the collection of hovels was an ancient place of suffering.

Sister Annis, with her tattered black robes and a face hidden beneath a ghostly veil, ruled over the lepers with an iron fist. Her heart darkened by the beheading of her cousin Elizabeth for soothsaying by Henry VIII, her severed head displayed cruelly upon a spike outside the Tower of London. An inferno of rage engulfed her being, her thirst for revenge becoming an insatiable hunger to punish the world. God was cast out from her soul.

Strangely as it seems and unexpectedly as time marched forward, an eerie transformation began to unfold within the leper colony. The sickly figures of the afflicted started to bear an uncanny improvement under Sister Annis's enigmatic care. Their gaunt faces filled out with life, their withered bodies strengthened, and they now wore well-worked animal skin clothes, mysteriously called pig suedes. When curious outsiders asked how this miraculous change came about, Annis would cryptically reply, "The King provided for us."

Beyond the colony's edge, an intricate network of secret underground tunnels sprawled, dug tirelessly by the lepers over generations to conceal their grotesque appearances from the world outside. These dark passages linked the colony to various locations, allowing the lepers to move like elusive shadows to obtain the necessities, but, hidden from prying eyes.

In this grim and twisted realm, young Sister Mary arrived, now Sister Annis had a devoted new helper. Young Sister Mary grappled with her own fears, but she loved to help the world with all her pure heart. One fateful day, a young woman, her clothes tattered, and body ravaged by a savage dog's bite in the forest, was brought by urgent necessity into their sanctuary. As Sister Mary tended to the woman's wounds, her eyes fell upon one particularly horrifying bite on the woman's thigh, the sinister shape of the letter "H" forever etched into her flesh, and Sister Marys memory.

Time passed, the young woman's bites healed, the deep H shaped one on her thigh being the last, and so she bade her farewells, leaving behind a shiver of unease that lingered in the air. Weeks later, during a solemn meal within the colony's hallowed halls, a peculiar incident occurred. As Sister Annis led the lepers in prayers, Sister Mary's thoughts wandered back to the scarred woman with the terrible dog bites.

For some reason or divinely prompted reason she opened her eyes during grace, and she recoiled in terror as an unspeakable realization struck like a bolt of lightning from a clear blue sky.

The joint of pork crackling on the table before her, ready to be carved and eaten by all, bore the same sinister "H" shape as had the scar on the woman's leg. Dread filled Sister Mary's heart as the shocking truth unravelled before her very eyes. The pig suede clothing was no animal skin at all, and the generous portions of roast pork were not what they seemed. Sister Annis and her lepers were not merely surviving on meagre means; they were insidiously cannibalizing the unsuspecting travellers who dared to pass through the treacherous woods of Danes Hills and Leicester Forest.

The revelation engulfed Sister Mary in a paralyzing horror, her world twisted beyond recognition. In this cursed haven of dark secrets, she found herself ensnared in a malevolent web of deception most evil, however, she had her wit about her, she somehow kept her head and managed to excuse herself from the table, she held herself together long enough, whilst knowing her very life depended upon outwards normality, all this whilst screaming to the rafters in her mind. She ran into the hills of Leicester Forest and into the moonless pitch-black darkness.

The shadows danced with sinister glee, in every bush she imagined a phantom, every tree seemed to have a face and the woods whispered their chilling secrets into her mind as she ran for her life, every bush she brushed was a gnarled hand grabbing at her as she tripped and stumbled her way to freedom where at last, she could tell the terrifying tale of sister Annis and her leper cannibals.

When the knights of the realm learned of the horrors that dwelled within the woods, they embarked on a perilous quest to rid the land of this vile menace. With swords held high and hearts resolute, they ventured into the darkness to confront the cannibal lepers and their wicked leader, the now newly named Black Annis.

The knights fought valiantly, facing unimaginable horrors as they tracked down the wretched creatures and they engaged in fierce combat. The caves echoed with the clash of steel, blood ran from the rock and the shadows danced with malevolence, but the knights were determined to prevail and put an end to the cannibalistic terror that had plagued the land for so long, many a spur was won beneath the ground at Danes Hills.

With great courage and skill, the knights managed to capture and defeat the cannibal lepers, the last of fighting took place on what is now the site of allotments on the Fosse Road/Groby Road junction and is still shown on maps as "Freaks Ground" on most maps, the cannibals twisted remains were burnt without ceremony. However, Black Annis, the ruthless and cunning leader, managed to evade capture, vanishing into the depths of the forest, forever eluding justice.

Though the cannibal lepers were defeated, the darkness cast by Black Annis endured. She became a haunting presence, lurking in the shadows, snatching unwatched children who strayed too far from safety. For three centuries, the people of Leicester Forest caught glimpses of her, whispered tales of her malevolence passing from generation to generation. Many believe she had turned to the dark arts and blood magic to cheat the reaper out of her death and live for evermore.

In the 1800s, as civilization encroached upon the once dense woods, the great trees had been felled and most of those left were pollarded to stumps each season, but the legend of Black Annis persisted. The Danes Hills bore witness to grand pageants where a cat, covered in aniseed oil to represent the scent of her lair, was chased by horse and hounds. The townspeople adorned themselves in their finest garments, and joyous revelry filled the air.

Yet, beneath the merriment, a haunting awareness lingered. Parents never allowed their children to wander alone or afar, for they could feel the ever-present spectre of Black Annis, the cannibal nun. The woods may have changed into New Parks Estate and houses built upon The Danes Hills, but her malevolence remains, a lingering shadow haunting the souls of all who know her name.

And so, the legend of Black Annis endured, a cautionary tale of the horrors that once lurked in the heart of Leicester Forest. Her legacy of fear and terror would forever serve as a reminder of the darkness that can dwell within even the most tranquil of places, a testament to the enduring power of folklore and the chilling tales of old.

2

The St. Johns Stone and its Long Shadow.

During the bronze age, some 5000 years ago a stone circle was being used by our ancestors, it could well be from the stone age. From these mysterious times there are whispers and echoes in writing from around the ancient worlds of the Greeks, Romans, and Carthaginians. Their words being written were of the Celtic druids, their rituals, and human sacrifices. The emergence of the druids in England predates all writings, they were the priests, their churches were the stone circles.

Leicester had a stone circle, it sat on the outskirts of the Celtic settlement of Ratae Corieltauvorum, what we now call Leicester. It possibly was not dissimilar to stone henge or other such circles. The centre piece could have been "The St John Stone." This was on the stadium estate near Parker Drive.

It was crescented by enigmatic stepped earthworks shaped like an amphitheatre's steps. Steps which possibly predated even the Roman era which were re-dug several times, the latest known refurbishment of the crescented steps and mysterious magical site was as late as 1800, but by whom and why?

The outer rings of the circle were gone long ago, leaving the St. Johns stone alone and even more magnificent and so demanding of a yarn....

St. John's Stone, drawn by a local artist, Miss Seema Solanki, interpreted using contemporary sources."

This stone had stood as a silent witness to the ebb and flow of time, its origins shrouded in the mists of antiquity and its birth into human cultures unknown. However, there are verbal echoes from the past of druids, about their forgotten rituals chants and incantations. These ancient earthworks hinted at a time when the land was young, and mystical energies danced freely across the landscape, they danced to the tunes the druids played.

Legends whispered of druids who once gathered around The St. John stone to conduct their sacred rites. They believed the stone possessed a unique connection to the spirits of the earth and heavens, a conduit for cosmic forces that shaped their world. The druids revered the stone, seeking guidance and wisdom from the divine through their rituals.

Yet, the tale took a dark turn when an evil druid, consumed by power and greed, sought to harness the stone's energies for his own sinister purposes. Driven by malevolence, he hatched a nefarious plan to desecrate the stone's purity and corrupt its divine connection.

In the depths of a moonless night, the evil druid committed a heinous act – he sacrificed a child, so pure of heart that her innocence shone like a beacon in the darkness. The gods were outraged by this wicked act, and in their wrath, they cursed The St. John stone, condemning it to carry the burden of the innocent girl's restless spirit forevermore.

From that moment on, an eerie pall settled over the stone, and whispers of the child's ghost haunting the amphitheatre spread like wildfire through the nearby settlements. Fearful tales of malevolent fairies and restless spirits became woven into the hearts and minds of the local people, leaving them haunted by the stone's dark past.

As the Victorian age dawned, the church, hearing rumours of supernatural occurrences and ghostly apparitions, decided to act. Fearing the lingering curse of The St. John stone, they conspired to remove it from its ancient resting place.

Under the veil of secrecy, the stone was transported to a secret location, a county church. There, masons, sworn to never reveal the stone's fate, were tasked with dismantling it to create altars, statues and fonts for churches across the shire.

But the curse, it seemed, could not be so easily undone. As the masons chiselled away at the once-pure stone, strange occurrences plagued them. Tools vanished without a trace, eerie whispers filled the air, and visions of the innocent girl haunted their dreams.

In their desperation to break the curse, the masons secretly turned to ancient texts and forgotten rituals from the books of their ancient order, seeking a way to appease the restless imprisoned spirit. In the depths of their toil, they rediscovered a long-lost rite, one that could set the young girl's soul free and lift the curse from The St. John stone.

With hearts heavy with remorse, the masons performed the blood magic rite, a solemn ceremony that freed the spirit of the pure-hearted child from within the stone prison. As the final incantation echoed through the night, a gentle sweet breeze swept through the church, carrying with it the faint sound of laughter, like the tinkling of bells.

From that day forth, the curse was lifted, and The St. John stone found peace. The legends of fairies and restless spirits faded into folklore, while the stone's true tale remained a dark macabre secret, known only to a select few.

And so, hidden within the churches across the city and shire, the once mysterious haunted stone, was now infused with the good spiritual energy of a child so pure, it began to shine and glisten with a radiant light, a symbol of hope and redemption in the face of darkness. The tale of The St John Stone lived on in the form of church alters and stone fonts made by the masons, one piece, said to be just up on the Hill in St. Lukes church, an enchanting reminder of the fantastical and mysterious history that is awash in the city and shire of Leicester.

St. John's Stone from contemporary sources by local artist Miss Seema Solanki.

3

Donkeys Years.

Meanderings of the Years of a Donkeys Ears. I Think!

As a native of Leicester, I as a child regularly visited Skegvegas and in my garage somewhere is an old shirt from one of many trips that reads "I am a chizzit and proud of it". For non-natives of Leicester reading this; Skegvegas is the seaside town of Skegness and a Chizzit is a holiday maker from Leicester who always asks "how much is it", due to our accent the shop keepers hear "chizzits". It has been donkey's years since I last went to "Skeggy" and a forthcoming trip got me to thinking about donkeys. I used to love going there for donkey rides as a child!

It has sprung to mind a story related to me in the garden, many discussions were had about the curious origins of the saying "donkey's years", you just read it without a thought as you know the saying so well even if it has been donkey's years since you heard it!

Within the audible sound of the Bells of St Mary le Bow in London lives a rather likable and peculiar type of Briton. The cockney, you can only be a cockney if when you were delivered into the world you were within the sound range of the mentioned bells. They have their own language, apples and pear equals stairs etc. and their example of a long passage of time is donkey's ears. "How long have you known him, Bill? "Oh for donkeys ears" is a probable reply. Cockney slang at its finest.

Another possible meaning of donkey's years is the cranes on the sides of riverside wharfs and railways were known as donkey cranes, the very early versions were very slow and its possible donkey's years is a crane operators' way of saying a long time, "How long till your unloaded Fred? "These donkeys take bloomin years". Could be dockers slang. Never has England been so proud of the Donkey Crane operators than when they turned their cranes and dropped their booms as Winston Churchills funeral barge passed them on the Thames.

However, a far more ancient and grizzlier story caught my attention. It seems to date back as far as the ancient Greeks and Romans, perhaps even Carthage itself. Who doesn't like ancient grizzly yarns.

I was chatting about grapevines when the yarn was spun that donkeys were thrown into a trench and then grapevines were planted on them. I had to look into that. Investigate I did and I asked my network of nonsense knowers, know-all's and weird trivia collectors and it was quite a picture they painted.

It seems there is credible evidence for the poor older donkeys' demise to feed the ancient world's lust for wines and grapes.

It would seem after a life of hard work one or a few of the older donkeys would indeed be dispatched. The ancients would dig a very long trench and fill it with water, once the water had soaked away a donkey would be bled out and its blood, innards and offal's would be spread out in the bottom of the trench. The new grape vines would be planted in the trench and the grape vines would be fed with iron rich and potassium filled soil for many years, donkey's years....

A secondary morsel of interest to do with this story was told of grapevines in the Victorian era. It seems the roots of the vine were often planted outside of the "glasshouse" in a hole in the ground with a few pints of blood making nutrient enriched soil, as the grapevine grew it was fed into a removed low window of the greenhouse where the fruiting and leafy part would grow (the leaves are edible and very desirable). This blood was also said to have fed the plant for donkeys' years.

So, there you have it you have been saying it for donkeys' years and you didn't even know!

4

The Gateway to Hell at Humberstone.

Sorry about the dramatic title, it's not an Iron Maiden song although the story is something of an echoing headbanger. There certainly are a lot of stories about the old humber stone that sits on the roundabout up near the Hamilton area of Leicester. While working in the garden people told me so many stories, I thought a re-visit was in order before I wrote this collection of fables surrounding it. I was not disappointed by my visit.

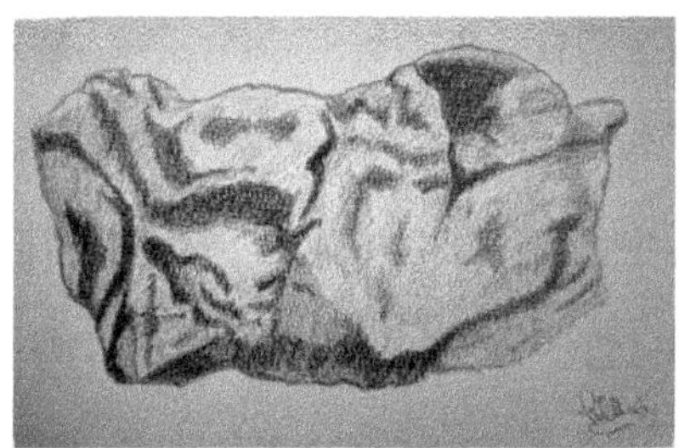

When I arrived it was a nice summers day and there was a fellow there who looked very grand and noble indeed. I did wonder what he was doing as I could hear the low murmur of either meditation or prayer emanating from his direction. To be honest he was more impressive than the stone at first glance. The stone is pretty much looking like a flat round stone no more than a foot high with a six feet diameter. This fellow looked like a kind of guru dressed in fine African style robes.

I waited by the fence, it seemed rude to go nearer. Once this fellow had finished and as he turned, he gave me a rather toothy friendly grin and I said "hello", and off the conversation went as it does. Turns out his name was Assan, and he was from a Nigerian tribe called "Igbo", he was most curious as to why I was writing this down and I informed him of this story, and he was most pleased to tell what he was doing and wanted it known.

It would seem he felt a spiritual need to send a prayer home and the stone was a channel, he informed me that there are thousands of these stones all across Europe and ancient Africans were able, through the use of telepathy to send messages home as they explored the world during the first great human migrations. The stones were a conduit of sorts into the mother earth. We chatted for quite some time, and it was a most pleasant hour and excited me to get on with the story of the stone.

The stone has not changed since my last visit, photographs do not do it Justice. Apparently in 1881 a Victorian science society dug to its bottom, it was ten feet high and shaped pentagonal. It also has very deep grooves in the top and is made of solid granite not seen anywhere for at least 6 miles and then some.

There are many well documented stories such as use as a Saxon sacrificial stone, self-combustion of crops near to it, ghosts, fairies, UFO's and goblins to name but a few.

However, I was most interested to hear why it is called Hells Stone. An adjacent field has always been known as Hells Hole Field. As the Vikings robbed and pillaged their way up the country they came to Leicester and the surrounding area led by two men called Scraper and Hubba. The villagers in the area who seem to have been numerous had many years before covered the entrance to a great cave in the hill with a great stone pulled across the land. The cave had been thought to be the entrance to hell and the stone, if kept clean and offered the right sacrificial inducements kept the devils in hell.

As Scraper, Hubba and their band got closer the villagers decided to open the gate to hell and let out the devils to fight the earthly devils. However, the devils cursed them for being held under the ground and joined and helped the Vikings as they burned and pillaged. Hubba was said to have stood on the stone and slain many Saxons, (Hubba, Humber, Hubbastone perhaps?) the Vikings took over the area and Scraper built his toft to live in, Scraptoft as we know it today. The locals killed or reduced to semi slaves. Hubba carried on with his army into the ancient kingdom of Wessex.

The cave story is interesting, the nearby Village of Humberstone has a beautiful Church, St Marys which was built in 1200ad over an ancient pagan site of worship. During the English civil war, a group of cavaliers was held prisoner in the church, surrounded by roundhead guards. To the amazement of the roundheads the cavaliers escaped, they were caught up near the great stone and swore on oath they had used a secret cave system they had stumbled upon, and all were frightened at seeing inside the caves with all manner of Hobbs creatures dwelling there and they were most pleased to be recaptured.

The stories of our island are varied and go back into the ancient depths of history to times even before the days when our history was recorded on velum skins by King Alfred the Great. There are oral stories of human sacrifices by druids, the goat headed ghosts, Hubba the Viking, goblins, druids, and even what people describe as UFOs around the stone.

Whatever the truth of our Humberstone, during the road widening around abandoned plague village of Hamilton adjoining the stone there are stories of the contractors removing in secret more great stones which formed a giant circle. In more recent year's archaeological digs have shown settlement and lots of human activity through the ages of modern man. Curiously to me personally they found flints worked by ancients in the stone age, perhaps the Nigerian holy man was right, the stone is a part of an ancient network of stones which could amplify telepathic thoughts from one stone to another around the world!

Artwork interpreted from contemporary sources by Miss Seema Solanki.

5

The Harking Holes of Glenfield and Beyond.

At the back of Mansion House on the Glenfield Hospital site where a great number of these yarns and stories were passed is a Victorian walled kitchen garden. Curious to the wall on one side are what most people would describe as arrow slits. Regular visitors to historic castles and fortifications may call them loopholes or the ancient name of crenels. In the context of a fortification or a castle this mayhap be true, for the firing of a bow, crossbow, or ballista etc.

In this instance however the holes face where a very old house stood, perhaps the original Frith House and possibly earlier houses and settlements which stood on the same footprint. Quite probably the secret garden started off as a vegetable plot for some woodsman in a thatched cottage who cleared a few trees in the Leicester Forest as it was known for as far back as the dark ages.

As the house developed a thicket would have been put around the clearing to keep out animals and the occasional villainous paupers passing by. Later a hawthorn hedgerow possibly cultivated around the growing foods. When the first substantial house appeared, the wall would have appeared in some form.

The holes in the wall are known in some places as harking holes or hailing's, it was said to me that there were strict hierarchies in some houses amongst the staff who worked them. Gardeners would never see the inside of some of the bigger houses. Produce would be taken to the tradesmen's entrance at the back or out of sight in some other way.

Likewise, footmen, maids and such would never think to enter a garden full of workmen. So, the need for easy communication without the meeting was solved with the harking holes. The cook of the house would send a message to the garden for some such things as a trug of parsnips or turnips and the hall boy or scullery maid messenger would hail through the hole for a gardener and relate the message to them never getting muddy shoes into the big house!

"Go hark at the gardeners for some parsnips for his Lordships dinner!"

6

A Fruity Fable.

Pound for pound one of the cheapest grown non-native fruits in British supermarkets is the humble but exotic looking pineapple. They are stacked high in the fruit and vegetable aisles, along with umpteen mixes of other fruits in the tin aisle and gallon after gallon available in all manner of drinkable forms.

We won't go to the sweet and cake aisle, a mention of pineapple cubes sweets is obligatory, a personal childhood favourite which gave me an excruciating decision between a quarter of a pound of them or the ever wink inducing rhubarb and custards, both left the roof of my mouth shredded but my goodness what a treat.

So, there we have it, pineapples are pretty much as cheap as can be. However, they weren't always. You may not believe it but I am about to tell you a story so fantastic you will think it's a child's story along the lines of Peter Pan or The Wizard of Oz, so let me lead you by the hand down the rabbit holes of your mind (with a pineapple on the table for dessert after the six o clock tea party).

Sailors around the old British Empire would come home with all sorts of yarns about their adventures to far flung places, the animals, fauna, and food. One particular fruit was so highly rated by them it reached the ears of Royalty and so the great ships of England all vied to be the first to bring a full cargo hold back to England. The fruit of course being the pineapple.

The sail ships would load their holds and put hard to the winds to reach England before the fruit perished. In the reign of Charles I, the race to grow our own was started after he was presented with one, apparently it is said it was the only one to make it from the whole shipload. His son King Charles II so taken by the fruit, upon being presented with the first homegrown pineapple he commissioned a painting to celebrate, and a botanical arms race was about to begin in the normally calm and tranquil walled kitchen gardens of England's finest houses and palaces.

The first problem of the day was making heat in the Pinery (yes, a greenhouse for growing pineapples is called a pinery but for ease on the ears we will say greenhouse). First, they tried the traditional greenhouse furnace method, but the smoke, soot and grimy air killed the plants! The next common attempt was to use lean to greenhouses with tall brick walls on one side, they lit fires and heated the wall to try to make it tropical inside, not a chance, so many walled kitchen greenhouses went up in flames the method was abandoned.

It became a mania in England to try to grow the elusive pineapple! Shipload after shipload of potted pineapple plants arrived and trundled inland on horse drawn wagons through the leafy lanes of England to the finest houses where the poor gardeners tried their best but killed them by the score during trial-and-error methods. It was an horticultural horror at the start.

If you know anything about England's incredible gardeners you know they will find a way, and find a way they did, albeit it in a rather strange but amazing way. Horse manure was the main answer to the heat problem.

Inside the greenhouses special floors were designed with cast iron grills of two feet square, and under these floors the steaming horse manure was placed, usually by the gardeners apparencies bless them, the manure was regularly turned, and the heat was almost perfect to generate "the tropics" suitable for growing the 17th century's king of fruits.

As you saw, almost perfect, and for the pineapple almost is not good enough. England's gardeners knew they were close. The answer came in the form of the humble flax seed, and the horses were about to get a nourishing treat! It was discovered that feeding horses boiled spelt and flax seed increased the heat of the manure they produced by just enough. A new industry was born, and the pineapple was about to induce a fruit mania within the aristocracy and gentry of England.

Such was the early difficulty of growing the pineapple when a fruit was ready to be eaten the great lord or titled estate owner would send out invitations to all the local bigwigs, dignitaries and wealthy. They would gather in the great dining rooms of the estates and gorge themselves on the finest foods in the land, an army of the poor toiling away below to feed the best to the few.

At the end of the meal the dignitaries would be given a pair of white gloves each, on each glove was the name of the fine house they were dining in and an embroidery of a pineapple. I personally believe the lady of the house and her daughters would have sewn these as a reminder for the guests of how clever and rich they are to have grown the fruit on their estate.

Then the moment would arrive, the head butler would walk in with the pineapple on a silver tray, dressed with all kinds of fauna and foliage to make it look as splendid as possible to the gasping and delighted guests, all around the bottom would be ready prepared local fruits of the highest quality.

The sight must have been most memorable, the pineapple was taken from the special pineapple holding dish that the great potters of the day were selling for these events. It was passed around the table, the nobles reduced to the like of peasants gawking into a great royal banquet, they would smell it, stroke it, hold it to the light and pass it to the next guest. The pineapple found its way safely back into the safe arms of the butler and the local fine fruits were offered to eat, but not the pineapple!

The bigwig who owned the pineapple would have several dinner parties to show off his pineapple, everyone of note would be invited to the event and the social ladder would be climbed to the top on the back of the exotic fruit. The amazing thing is that the pineapple would travel many a mile after these dinners, albeit in a downwards social journey......

The pineapple was such a valuable item, often if would be sold, in a shop specialising in nothing but pineapples and their accoutrements, and at any given time the pineapple shop may have but one or two in stock. Such was its value when the pineapple was taken to the shop to be sold it would be accompanied by two large strong men from the estate to prevent its theft. There are estimates that a single pineapple was as valuable at a large family house in a town.

Our pineapple would then be purchased by the next class down, perhaps a wealthy merchant who has risen to the upper middle classes. He would have dinner parties for all his newly established middleclass friends. But, again, not a bite or slice was to be had!

The pineapple would end up so bruised, battered, and old that it would end up a mush inside and not even edible more oft than not.

The pineapple mania finally ended with the faster steamships who were able to get them to the British tables before they were rotten, and to the horror of the gentry and ballooning snobbish middle classes the working class began to eat them which really was not acceptable!

You would think, with the country houses littered and decorated with such things as pineapple newel posts on stairs, pineapple bedposts, pineapple broaches, even a huge stone building shaped like one at Dunmore, and anything you can care to think of, this mania would have taught the wealthy a good lesson.

Not a chance, like the ticktokkers, Instagrammers and influencers of today they moved on to the next madcap thing, celery. A verbatim botanical and social arms race with celery began the same as the pineapple!

Artwork by Jevgenija Zulfugarova.

7

The Flesh Eating Blackberrys of Gelsmore (sort of).

People of a certain age will have the fondest memories of blackberry picking with their relatives, at the very least memories of picking with friends or siblings whilst out playing, then returning home with purple lips to questions from your mother as to why you also have a stained shirt and probably the trots!

I did both the above, I was fortunate enough during the school holidays to spend my early years at Aqueduct Cottage in the tiny hamlet of Gelsmoore near Coalville with my grandparents, Reg, and Ethel Baker, it was like traveling back in time 150 years. They made all kinds of things from nature, lots with blackberries and I am proud of them when I say, "they were proper country folk who make do n mend, pickled and preserved". Everyone knows you can make jam from these purple pearl clusters of deliciousness, but did you know you can make blackberry vinegar which is a wonderful medicine for chesty coughs, a cure for gout or a dye for cloth (you ought to know this from your school shirt so badly stained as a child). There are of course blackberry wines, cakes and I could write for hours on many a use or benefit of this cousin of the beautiful rose!

However, I write to warn you of the dangers of blackberries, their thorns are notorious. They can grow up and above an inch of hard as steel leather piercing daggers. <u>They also like to eat meat!</u>

Mornings in the hamlet started with a small forage along the abandoned, old overgrown redundant Stephenson railway bank. We would be picking all manner of items of salad like dandelion leaves, fungi such as chicken of the wood, elderberries, and various roots, just enough for the day, each day! Grandad Reg always had a story. I liked the one where he said, “they were so poor in that area they couldn’t afford a steam engine to pull the coal wagons along that stretch of the ole Swanny line”. (I recently found it seems true, the coal wagons were pulled by horses on the tracks in this area). This day's story in the mornings misty coal smoke filled air was a warning to young children everywhere. Blackberries eat meat and they like to eat silly young children who reach too far into the blackberry bushes for the juicy ones at the top! That got my attention as a child.

When you look at various types of thorned plants the spikes generally stick out to repel anything that may eat them. Not the blackberry bush, the blackberry bush has thorns designed to stop anyone caught up from getting away, esp. small children in woolly jumpers, you just know many a medieval peasant maid in heavy woolly clothing was grabbed by these triffids to be slowly digested by the earth at the base of the bush.

I have asked and looked into this old fable, it would seem some gardeners regard the blackberry bush as a meat eater, small sheep, woolly pigs (they are naturally a very hair animal with long very dark hair which domestication has bred out of them to the pink bloaters we know today) and native goats to our islands have for centuries munched away on the blackberry bush bounty, but oft they stray a little close, they reach in for the bait, those hard to get big juicy ones, and that's it. The thorns go into the thick fur, the more the hapless creature wriggles the more thorns go into the fur and tentacle like stems of the bush envelope enough to hold the prey in place like a giant octopus overpowering a sea galleon.

The animal tires, time passes, the poor creature succumbs to the blessing of death, then the bush begins to feed as the hapless creature disperses its body back to the earth through decomposition, the animal carcass will feed the blackberry bush and a million creatures in its root system for many a year. This is a feast of nutrients released for many years.

So, my Grandads yarn about the meat eating blackberry bushes of Gelsmore was mostly true, the only untrue part was that it only happened in Gelsmore, it happens everywhere, many a farmer has found sheep missing and just recovered a few tufts of fur. Makes you wonder when you see a piece of cloth hanging in a blackberry bush.........

Artwork by Jevgenija Zulfugarova.

8

What Lies Beneath.

No written work about Leicester and the surrounding shire could possibly be complete without a clock tower mention. It has a sort of proper official name, The Haymarket Memorial Clock Tower, it was designed by Joseph Goddard and erected in 1868 after fundraising amassed the princely sum of just over £2000 pounds odd and ninepence. All the other information on its construction is available in a myriad of wonderful places and sources. I will also omit all well-known facts and information from its early days with the exception of small factual smorgasbord for your imagination to feast upon. Two of the unusual things to me are Lady Jane Grey was almost on a plinth instead of Simon De Montfort, but the one weird fact that still surprises most, The Hitler Youth once paraded in front of it, saluted it and then promptly marched off up London Road and set up a Nazi camp complete with swastika flags, a weird oddity I simply had to include.

There are some other interesting opinions about the clock tower, one is its ability to move a town, well a slight exaggeration, but to move the centre of activity of a town. Leicester lost its official city status centuries ago and at the time of construction of the clock tower Leicester was still a town, becoming an official city properly only in 1919.

The town of Leicester during the Victorian era was a bustling place, the most central point of meeting and of the most important business was mostly in the High Cross area, in what we know today as Jubilee Square. The streets around the guildhall and church of St Martins (now the Cathedral) have more or less had the same layout even to this day, the road and street layout would actually be familiar to an ancient Roman, it was a thronging place of business and commerce. During the early years of the 1800's the Haymarket area was a bit of a pound shop area to be brutal, there was even a "muck hill". You can imagine, the area was busy, dirty, smelly and dangerous due to the many horse drawn vehicles, the land and property value was not as prime as around the Guildhall and High Cross St.

Enter a group of clever enterprising businessmen, led I believe by one of those newfangled cutting-edge photographers, and so, The East Gates Improvement Consortium was formed, and it was on a mission. Conveniently and funnily enough they were mostly all based around the area where the clock tower would later be built, oh what luck! They campaigned and fundraised hard to raise the money, raise it they did. The best thing they did for their consortium was raise the value of the land they owned around the clock tower, and they also raised the footfalls into their businesses. That is how you move a town centre and, in the process, make yourself very wealthy with the gift of a 70ft high watch as a sweetener!

Construction began. There is a very well-known picture of the clock towers foundation stone being placed by a group of stove pipe hatted dignitaries, since the day of that stone being placed it's regularly been in the newspapers, multiple history books and all manner of pamphlets. It is almost always lauded as the first stone in the construction of Leicester's wonderful tower like a religious fever akin to the Turin shroud or a fragment of the true cross of Calvary.

Sorry to disappoint, but underneath the clocktower are brick lined vaults and a three large man-made brick sewer canals. Just 17 paces in the direction of Belgrave from the tower are a secret set of well-worn Portland stone steps leading deep down into a huge cavern, vaulted like the ceiling of a castle, and on top of this vaulting directly above this man-made canal is the "foundation stone of the clock tower". I know it is true as I have been down there in the 1970's and seen them with my own eyes!

I don't know where those canal/sewers/tunnels go, but everyone knows the city and county is home to a vast maze of tunnels, often from church to church and abbey to abbey, my personal favourite being the Ashby Castle tunnel. I think when we tested Richard III's DNA we should have tested the people of Leicester to see what percentage of mole they contain! Even with all that has been said, I do love our iconic Clock Tower and anyone who has been a long-term citizen will have a clutch of clock tower stories of their own!

9

A Pressing Story.

Roman Leicester was a decent sized city, looking at what remains to this day almost 2000 years later it must have been a bustling town. When they first came, they overpowered, subjugated, or cajoled the local Britannic kings of the Corieltauvorum. They may have simply absorbed anyone of note and Romanised them. Leicester (Ratae) still has some very large Roman ruins and a recent find under the Cathedral extension is a Roman temple of some note. The legend of the temple under the Cathedral has been passed down orally for hundreds of years, now they have found it and proved the value of oral testimony I do hope they find the pagan place of worship they say The Romans built their temple over as a sign of dominance! Leicestershire's history truly is like peeling an onion.

In more distant parts of what the Romans called Britannia local kings and queens at a more tribal level entered into treaties and agreements. Life had settled down for many after the invasion by Rome in AD43, however, Roman laws and tribal traditions did clash from time to time, but it was generally local and easily dealt with by the Romans.

Around AD60 a northern tribe, the Iceni was mourning the death of their king when a contingent of Romans arrived. The Romans demanded taxes, tribute, and a share of the dead kings' lands in duty. The king's daughter and granddaughters tried to express their case to rule as per local custom, Britannia was quite accustomed to queens. The new queen is well known in British folklore as Bodicia, (Bouddica) queen of the northern tribe of the Iceni.

The Romans became drunken and abusive, several people were murdered and Boudica and her daughters were dragged away by the Romans and horribly mistreated. The Romans took their booty, fired the tribal capitol, and went off on their drunken way. Little did they know what they had started in their drunken debauched foray.

As word spread around the north of the mistreatment of a royal family, the normally warring tribes of Britannia began to assemble as allies, Queen Bodicia was on the warpath, and she was drawing in tens of thousands of warriors from many tribes. Bodicia set off to the large city of Colchester where the city was burnt to the ground and plundered with anyone Roman put to the sword, anyone not on Bodicia's side was massacred. The city was so thoroughly burnt down there is said to be a foot of ash just below ground level to this day.

The great tribes joined, including the Corieltauvorum. which were widespread in Leicestershire, guerilla tactics ensued giving the ancient Britons victories large and small, London was burnt and sacked, St Albans put to the sword as Bodica and her warriors wrought revenge through fury and flame.

In AD61 many warriors had returned home to tend crops and rearm when news came of a great Roman army which had marched inland from Wales. The Romans had just attacked and captured the religious heartland of Celtic Britannia, Anglesey, killing hundreds of druids. Outraged, once again the Britons started to gather in great numbers, all eager after the previous conquests and the booty that comes with victory. Bloodlust overtook and so began the great gathering of the tribes, encouraged by the remaining druids.

They started to gather and march along the Roman roads and converged on the Fosse Way, imagine 80.000 blue painted warriors and their war chariots marching along Melton Road and the Golden mile of Leicester! The Romans marched along Wattling Street to meet them, they met over in nearby Warwickshire close to the Roman fort at Manchetter, and what was to unfold would shape the nation.

80.000 Britons of all the great tribes gathered in front of a professional modern army of ten thousand armour clad Romans. The druids out in front were chanting their curses and incantations. The Celtic people of Britannia, many painted blue with woad, covered in traditional tattoos were set to attack. Legend and folklore tell of hundreds of war chariots, Led by Bodica of the Iceni, with swords on the wheel axels hurtling towards the Roman lines and cutting down swathes of Romans whilst hurling spears and arrows into them.

The terrible truth is the tribal leaders had no concept of fighting such a modern army, 80.000 Britons whipped up with blood lust by the druids and hate fuelled oaths of vengeance hurled themselves at the Romans. The Romans had chosen the battlefield wisely so the Britons could not outflank them. As the throngs of thousands pressed hard against the Roman shields, each Roman soldier was trained to stab from behind his shield to the front of the men to his right with his perfectly balanced gladius sword. Over his shoulder a lance would be jabbing back and forth into the trapped throng of Britons, on command the Romans switched with the men behind, so the Britons faced rested troops continually, the slaughter was dreadful. The saying "hard pressed" was born into common language, the front Britons so hard-pressed from behind against the Roman shields they could not raise their weapons to even fight or defend themselves.

The battle is known as "The Battle of Watling Street". It is, unfortunately for the Britons, a wonderful example of a well-trained, well-disciplined, and well-armed modern army, using well-honed tactics to defeat incredible numerical odds. The remnants of the Britannic army scattered back to their homes. Bodica and her daughters, fearing capture took poisons concocted by the druids.

The Romans soon recovered, and if one thing most people known about the Romans is they have a fearful reputation for vengeance. News was sent to Rome, many Romans were at first horrified at the sacking of their cities, but also horrified at the treatment of a great royal family albeit a tribal one. More troops were still sent with demands for retribution.

As the Romans advanced through the country, dispensing their retribution, they reached the region of Leicestershire. Here, the once resilient

Corieltauvorum tribe faced a swift defeat, their leaders falling victim to Roman might, either through death, ransom, or hefty fines. A significant portion of the local populace found themselves enslaved, tasked with the arduous labour of reclaiming the soggy lowlands of the magnificent Soar Valley. Roman engineers forced them to dig intricate land drains into the marshy terrain, this channelled the excess water into the River Soar, effectively transforming the once waterlogged lands into habitable areas of productivity.

Today, old formerly bogged and marsh areas such as the Martins Grove (now Belgrave) Thurmaston and many low-lying areas in the valley are still serviced by these drains put in almost two thousand years ago. When Rushey Mead estate was built the Roman land drains were still working and as foundations were dug through them, they were repaired to keep the area dry. There have also been a good many remains found of Celts, the latest being three bodies recovered from the foundations of an extension being dug on Jacklin Drive.

There is also still a Roman presence in the area, Thurmaston footpath is said to be haunted by the ghost of a lone Roman sentry, and in the depths of Charnwood Forest, beneath the trees, a haunting spectacle has been seen. A legion of Roman soldiers has emerged several times, their ghostly figures marching in formation. Their uniforms are said to hang in tatters, echoing the decay of time. Haggard faces with hollowed eyes bear the weight of an eternity of ghostly battles. Having not seen them myself I would be hard pressed to believe it.......

10

You Wooden Believe It!

India is a wonderful, fantastical and in many ways a mysterious country even to the residents of Leicester who share a colourful history with India and its peoples in a myriad of ways. As a resident of the Belgrave and Rushey Mead most of my life I know a thing or two about India, its culture, religions, and all manner of its wonders.

Indulge me on this that I found so interesting. If you have a tree growing on your land in India, probably with the exception of The Punjab region, you will need to call in a tree wallah. Think of the expense!

Well no, that's not the case, amazingly in India if you need a tree taken down you call in the tree wallah (woodcutter), he will give you a price for the work and it is you who gets the money! They not only cut down your unwanted tree, but they also cart it off and pay you handsomely for the wood!

From what people have told me, not so much as a twig is wasted!

11

The Green Lady of Belgrave.

In the forgotten corners of Belgrave, Leicester, a tale of tragedy and a restless spirit is whispered from the lips of the residents of "Dummy Town". It sends chills down the spines of those who dare to tread the old pathways of the village. So, to the tale of a Belgrave spectre. It is from not so long ago, in a time when the village thrived on the lifeblood of its canals, whence did live there a lock keeper and his wife, Sophia.

Sophia was a woman of vibrancy and beauty, with flowing auburn hair and eyes that held a glimmer of mystery. She was the beloved wife of Mathew, the lock keeper whose duties kept him away busy for long stretches of time. Sophia's days were often spent in maintaining their large brood of loved children, attending to the lock keeper's cottage and its surrounding grounds, awaiting her husband's return.

It was on a fateful twilight eve one January when darkness had begun to blanket the river and moorings that tragedy struck. Sophia, donned in her heavy woollen garments, made her way along the lock, her footsteps muffled by the silence of the night. As she stepped onto a slippery patch near the lock edge, her world shifted beneath her feet, and with a harrowing cry, she plummeted into the icy embrace of the river.

The frigid waters closed around her, swallowing her desperate pleas for help. Sophia's heavy clothing, once a shield against the biting chill, became an anchor, dragging her deeper into the abyss. Gasping for air and reaching out with trembling hands, she cried out in anguish, "Mathew! Mathew!"

But Mathew, unaware of his wife's perilous plight, was absent, consumed by his duties and unaware of the passage of time. As Sophia's strength waned, her voice grew faint, being swallowed by the roily depths of the river. Each call for her beloved became a quitter whisper, a plea for salvation in a world that had turned deaf to her cries. "Mathew, Mathew."

In her final moments, Sophia succumbed to the icy grip of the water, and she swore an oath as she was drowning, that she would not leave this place until Mathew saved her, he didn't save her mortal body. Sophia became bound by oath to this realm, transformed into a ghostly figure surrounded by the green swirling waters. She haunts the old areas of Belgrave, forever enshrouded in that swirly green mist that dances eerily in the moonlight.

As dusk settles over the village, casting long shadows across the ancient St Peters church walkway, the Ghost of the Green Lady often emerges from the spectral depths. Her mournful figure glides silently along the worn cobblestones and between the gravestones, her eyes haunted by the echoes of lost love. The soft whisper of her voice drifts through the night, carrying her eternal yearning for Mathew into the depths of the living world.

Many of those who have dared to wander the quite church walkway claim to have glimpsed her ethereal form, a spectral beauty veiled in a green mist. They speak of a palpable sorrow that clings to the air and penetrates to the bone, an otherworldly presence that sends shivers cascading down their spines. And in the twilight's embrace, they hear her gentle call carried upon the breeze, a melancholic plea that resonates with the deepest chambers of their hearts. "Mathew, Mathew."

12

Are you a Beanie Belly?

A little wigwam of beans planted in the secret garden project at Glenfield hospital in Leicestershire by the volunteer gardeners sparked more than a few bean stories. I had no idea beans were such a big deal, for Leicestershire in particular. The village place names alone such as Barton in the Beans, Beanfields, Beanley, Beanhill and Beans Norton are an indication of something unusual about the shire.

Apparently, beans, broad ones usually in the case of Leicestershire were pretty much regarded as a crop grown for animal feed. However, the people of Leicestershire started eating them for themselves. It became such a localised thing that during the medieval era there was a fun saying, "Shake a Leicestershire man by his collar and you will hear the beans rattle in his belly as he laughs".

Broad beans (vicia faba) seem to have been the favourite by a large margin. It is quite ironic that all these place names have bean in their names when broad beans are not actually a bean, they are a type of pea, that being said, I am still happy and proud to be a beanie belly and if you shake me, I will indeed laugh and probably rattle a little!

13

The Birds Nest in the new parks.

Birds Nest Avenue, on New Parks Estate, conjures up an image of a fine stick-built nest high in a tree, home to maybe a crow or a magpie. You would think there was a tree with such a nest before the builders got there in the mid 1950's. But that's not how it got its name, and its history is ancient and quite interesting.

The Danes reached Leicestershire around 865. The combined great heathen army overwhelmed local Kings across the island, and the country was divided up. Leicester itself became part of Danelaw. Names such as Ivor the Boneless, Guthrum and Ragnor Lothbrock became part of our national history.

Even all these tens of centuries later, long after the Danes left, we today still call the area where they lived Dane Hills. But they did not camp in tents!

They built a stronghold which was surrounded by a great high mound of earth; topped on the mound were spiked wooden palings. Not too far away was Gynn's Hall (modern day Gynsills).

Inside this great works was an enormous timber tower, reaching high into the sky. Again, atop were palings. It was built to watch over the locals who had been conquered. From afar the giant watch tower looked as if it were a bird's nest. The place became known as "The Birds Nest" to the inhabitants of the local settlement of Leicester and the surrounding area. Over 1100 years later the name still stands.

The Danes were pushed out in 919 and those who stayed were integrated into the new Kingdom. Inside the Kingdom power needed to be consolidated and no doubt the Birds Nest stronghold would have been used. It was not until 954 that the last Viking, Erik Bloodaxe, was driven from the fledgling country of England.

The next time the Birds Nest comes into historical view is 1378. There are various reports about the condition of the already old stronghold. It was being used as a hunting lodge for the extensive

Leicester Forest. Four men were employed to work on and repair the buildings: Robert Ireland, Robert Hod, Adam Gryst and William Redford. It's nice that their names are remembered.

The roofs were given slate covering as opposed to thatch and wood shingles. The moat was also dug out again to a depth of eight feet and 28 feet across, which would have been quite a task to say the least.

In 1526 it was being used as a hunting lodge, albeit a well-fortified one. A draw-bridge had been added along with other defences. All manner of nobility from the house of Lancaster were hunting in The Leicester Frith Deer Park. Later that year the park was split, and two new deer parks were added. (Yes reader, new parks!).

So, there you have it. The next time you see a nest in a great tree or walk along Birds Nest Avenue or see the remaining earthworks next to the New Parks working Men's Club: think of the giant tower in the stronghold, once lost amid the midst of time but now alive again in your mind.

14

The Chattering Lady of Mansion House.

Mansion House on the Glenfield Hospital Site in Leicester is a well know feature, it is not old as one would think, it was built in 1870 for local cotton factory owner Thomas Swift Taylor and his family. At the back of the house is a two-story stone bay window which at the middle on the inside is a semi gothic hardwood staircase with a large turn, a landing, with enough room for a small table and a couple of comfortable fabric covered chairs.

The view from the window is amazing, looking out for miles across Anstey and Bradgate towards the ancient Bradgate deer park. The light dances in through the Victorian handmade glass giving off a myriad of patterns in the gallery and the turn on the stair.

It is on this stair turn in the light where one of the young ladies of the house liked to sit and read, Nellie would often beckon a passing servant or maid to sit and listen to her read from the latest novels, laughing and giggling would ensue, or gasps of fear at stories from Penny Dreadfuls, no doubt often getting the said recipients of her readings a good scolding afterwards by a more senior member of staff.

During the mid-1880's fever spread through Leicestershire, and it took Nellie along with it, snatched in her youth. The house and all within were devastated at the loss of her bubbly and bright character.

However, that was not the last they would hear of Nellie, many a time in the hundred and thirty odd years since the fever took her, staff working in Mansion House have heard laughter and chattering on the turn of the stairs on a sunny day. They hear running and laughter in the gallery, so often so that Nellie is now known as "The Ghost of the Chattering Lady".

15

The Tempestuous Coronation Day at Osgathorpe.

Nothing ever happens in sleepy Osgathorpe, quietly muttered by almost every resident since the year dot. It is a little village nestled into a camouflage of hedgerows, fields, humps, bumps, hills, and hollows in the landscape of Leicestershire. It is so quiet they say they did not even put any water in the canal they dug out nearby! That's not to say it is not quaint and beautiful in the way English villages are.

The most remarkable thing about Osgathorpe is how unremarkable it is. The little village, nestled and tucked away near the ancient Grace Dieu priory has never had more than a couple of dozen houses at most with even those not always occupied. Life has ebbed and flowed from what I can find albeit in a general happy but uneventful manner for scores of centuries, even exempt from any proverbial bumps in the night and the like, even the ancient church, with one exception, there is maybe one story of note.

The year was 1660, Cromwell stood down the most ferocious fighting force Europe had ever seen, The New Model Army, he also stepped down as Lord Protector, and on the 2nd day of June Charles II was restored to the throne of England, the Bishops went back into parliament, and you didn't guess anything at all correctly as sleepy Osgathrope missed it all, as was the norm!

However, this was not to be a normal sleepy day for the village, the peasants were in the fields, the birds chirping in the trees and the cows chewing the cud, so serene. Then it came, from out of nowhere, a great wind of tornados and in it was half of the neighbouring village of Worthington, swirling in the air, cows, villagers, windmill blades and even a man still sitting in the saddle of his hoss as if riding the storm like one of the four hossmen of the apocalypse. Osgathorpe was about to feel the wrath of God.

The church was hit, houses and barns flattened or taken clear away, the orchards wrecked, and fields of crops flattened or blown into the sky, by the mercy of lady luck no one was hurt, not even the fellow on the "hoss" was hurt. Hoss of course being the proper pronunciation for horse in the area. I say not hurt, into the winds were reaped a dozen beehives with all their thousands of bees, lost and rudderless the bees did sting a few villagers.

The people ran into their thatched cottages and prayed, as the rain in the storms pounded their little stone cottages the animals hiding and sleeping in the thatching's of the roof began to fall out in shock, some already wet through. From the thatching fell all the dogs of the villagers and the pungent polecats (a smelly weasel like creature now about extinct that gave the expression of “stinks like a polecat”) from where they usually slept, the cry went to the rafters from the terrified villagers of “It’s raining cats and dogs”!

So next time you put your brolly up in a rainstorm and say to yourself “It’s raining cats and dogs” spare a thought for the little sleepy village and their endurance of the great storm of 1660 to bring you this now common little phrase we all say with such ease!

A ditto to the village.

In the village of Osgathorpe, a tempest arose, the winds howled fiercely, and the trees arose. With thunderous might, the skies turned dark, Osgathorpe trembled, like a tiny ark.

Amidst the chaos, the villagers stayed, facing the tempest, undismayed. Thousands of bees buzzed in the storm, Yet Osgathorpe's spirit remained warm.

On the day King Charles II took the throne, Osgathorpe's strength and courage were shown. "Cats and dogs, it may rain," they proclaimed, But Osgathorpe so sleepy will remain.

Wonderful Artworks by local artist Pammie Raymond.

16

The Great Stork Derby of Torornto.

Whilst I know this story is not local, it still fascinated me and in the voice of Verruca Salt, it's my book so I am including it. For many reasons The Great Stork Derby should never have been allowed to happen and I must be honest, I do not think we can say for sure it would not be allowed to happen again even in this modern age of multimedia and its thirst for clicks and viewers.

The story starts in 1926 with the death of a very eccentric lawyer who was also a well-known serial practical joker. Charles Millar left an estimated $2.2 million dollars to the woman who could produce the most children in the ten years following his death. The newspapers went wild, and it was dubbed the Great Stork Derby and when the story hit England it was called The Great Stork Race.

There was an immediate uproar from conservative groups and a challenge to the will was issued to the courts, the courts found in favour of Millar and the race was on to produce the most babies in a decade for a life of unbridled wealth. Again, the papers went into a frenzy.

A person might make the mistake of thinking ten, a baby each year, but there are nine months to a year, and what of multiple births such as twins and triplets, what of still born and miscarriages, would they count? What of the outrageous thought of children out of wedlock? The courts had to decide again and by the time the courts ruled there were a clear group of eleven families in the running, each with the press following their every move to feed the greedy fire of the story.

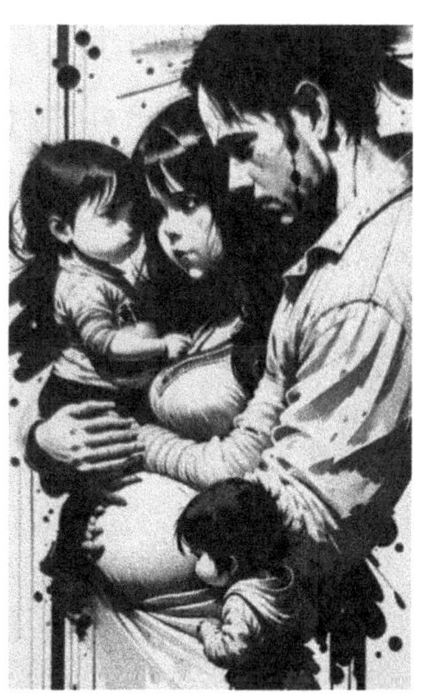

Within the first three years seven families were either disqualified or out of the running. Soon there were only four families and after the ten years each family or woman had nine bouncing babies each.

Once again it went back to the courts for them to try to sort it all out, the papers were wild on the story and every newspaper had dedicated reporters. This was also the golden age of the wireless radio, crowds gathered around to listen to the reports as they were giving out live updates as the courtroom battle swayed back and forwards as though it were a boxing match.

In the end the courts decided the four families which all had nine babies were equal winners, the sting in the tail was the cost of all the legal costs which took a mass of Millars fortune, four women earlier disqualified were given a token amount to “shut up”. There was unfortunately for the families a real surprise, the state of Toronto claimed back all the welfare and benefits they had paid out to the women for their children. Millar the practical joker had his rather ugly twisted last laugh as the families ended up with practically nothing financially!

Brewery image permission use kindly granted by The Muddy York Brewing Co, Canada.

17

The Lord of the Lake and His Quest for The Black Gold.

During the mid 1700's or there abouts, Lord Winstanley of Braunstone Hall was having a few issues with money, so he set about trying to think of innovative ways he could raise funds. He tried all sorts of things, but one of them can only be described as madcap. There was little income from the estate and its upkeep was crippling financially, so desperate times required desperate measures. A few years later and money would be abundant, but not yet!

At this time Braunstone Hall lay in a very rural area, nothing like it is today. It was bordering to the old village and liberty of Bromkinsthorpe, (people from the Westcotes area were called "Bromkins" for many a generation by the townsfolk of Leicester) all now swallowed up by the vast housing estate of Braunstone and earlier Victorian Westcotes area.

Somehow Lord Winstanley concluded that there was coal under his land, all hands available were set to digging, all manner of people from the estate were employed on the dig. It is said even the houseboys and maids played their part in the dig for coal! Dig they did, a vast pit was bored deep into the earth.....

This venture did not go unnoticed, the colliers (miners) over in the Coalville area were non too happy to hear of a possible coal mine so close to the city. So, they decided to put a stop to it and protect their already meagre livelihood.

The miners came in a large mob, old drays and all manner of carts with men loaded on, some even say the mob was led by a man who rode a large horned bull. When they arrived at the Winstanley coal dig a mass fight ensued between the estate men and the miners.

The miners gave the estate men a good beating and saw them off, the miners then placed explosives of gunpowder around the great pit and set the fuse. There is a story of valet being killed in the explosion and his ghost still haunts Winstanley House. The miners then rolled great boulders and rocks into the hole and made good their escape into the night.

The damage was done, the mining venture left in ruins. However, the story of the pit does not end there. It is said the lake on Braunstone Park is the remains of the day the lord went mining for black gold and many locals swear they still see a ghostly figure of a valet emerging from dark lakes and walking to Braunstone Hall.

18

What did The Normans ever do for us.

1066, apart from probably being the pin number to your bank account (the only possible alternative being 1966 for anyone over 50), is a number etched into the minds of almost every child raised in England. It of course relates to the Battle of Hastings where King Harold Godwinson took an arrow in the eye and England was lost, The Norman conquest was complete, we were now occupied by William of Orange, his barons, and lords, more or less. The weird thing is how many of the initial invaders ancestors still have hereditary seats in the house of Lords, but that's for another time and place.

Alas there is a body blow to your history teacher, Harold did not actually get an arrow in the eye, he was butchered on the field after taking a lance, six knights led by The Duke of Orange, killed him, beheaded his corpse, chopped him up and removed the delicate parts that made him a man. "The Bayeux Tapestry" you cry, to which I reply, "The one made under the eyes of the victorious Normans?"

We should acknowledge deservedly the fight that was put up by King Harolds army. As Harold waited for the Norman invasion which he expected from the English Channel, a huge Viking invasion took place in the north of the kingdom, and they captured York! King Harold marched his men, with all their kit and equipment thirty to forty miles a day to cover the almost two hundred miles. A feat still argued and debated about, but admired and respected.

The huge ferocious Viking army expected an easy win, but Harold and his men gave them an utter thrashing at Stamford Bridge in Yorkshire which resulted in a complete defeat which practically left all the Vikings dead. The Viking army had arrived in three hundred ships, they only managed to take between eight and twenty ships home (the ancient chronicles are varied) which even then the ships were sparsely crewed! It was noted for over fifty years after the battle there were bones and skeletons littering the battlefield such was its ferocity.

The battle is known for the big-name Vikings who were killed, as well as King Harolds treasonous brother, I will not name them all. However, there is a Viking, who is believed to have been a berserker (yes, that's where it comes from when you go berserk, a fierce out of control blood lusted Viking warrior), who's name we do not know. He stood alone on the narrow footbridge at the site of the battle of Stamford, he fought off the English army on the narrow bridge with a sword and an axe.

According to the chroniclers he killed and wounded forty English before a sneak spearman swam under the foot bridge and speared him in his previous evening's dinner. This brave man, even though he was an enemy and we do not know his name, deserves a mention for his bravery and valour.

The thing Harold did here, apart from beating the huge Viking army, was the march he, his men, their equipment and all their needs had made. They covered two hundred miles, many on foot in just an astonishing four days. It is a march admired by infantry soldiers even to this day, that aside from the battle! It is worth this second mention as it was such a deed.

Three days after the battle; news reached King Harold of the expected Norman invasion in down in Sussex led by William of Orange, The Duke of Normandy. King Harold turned his army south and three weeks later the Battle of Hastings took place nowhere near Hastings! England fell to the Normans after a heroic fight, the legend and fable of King Harold being killed by an arrow to the eye was literally sewn into our history so I will not go into great details about the battle.

I will say, Harold had a fight on his hands as many of the great estates of England had been purchased, acquired by marriage, or gifted by previous kings to Norman nobles who fought at the battle against King Harold.

During the battle a fellow of whom the people of Leicester and the shire would come to know came to prominence. Hugh De Grendmesnil, known as Hugo. He was a favourite of William of Orange, he supplied most of the great war horses for the invasion of England.

During the battle, De Grendmesnil, aloft one of his great war horses was at a charge when his reins snapped, his horse ran at a hedgerow and jumped it, right into a mass of English foot soldiers who all started jabbing at him with a great clatter of steel onto armour, somehow Hugh held on, his horse had the good sense to turn around and jump out of the melee back over the hedge to safety. Amazing horse and amazing horsemanship!

As was the custom the lands conquered were spoils and as such divided up by the winning king. Newly crowned William the Conqueror gave great swathes of land to Hugh De Grendmesnil, including Leicester and the surrounding shires. Leicestershire had a new lord and he came to claim his spoils. The people of Leicester gave resistance; however, we were overcome and subjugated.

Hugh De Grendmesnil started fortifying his lands quickly, he is credited with building the first Leicester Castle which is behind and next to the almost 2000-year-old Jewry wall, you just know they ripped down a lot of it for its stone when it was a mere 1000 years old! What did the Normans ever do for us?

Well to be fair, the Normans did a lot, they started constructing great churches, Cathedrals, and fortifications which we regard these days as English. Then there is the matter of one of the most important books in English history, The Doomsday Book, and one of its primary contributors was none other than Leicester's now very own Hugh De Grendnesmil!

After over a thousand years of Norman blood on our throne we can also be pleased that the next King, after King Charles III will be King William and he is full of Saxon Spencer blood. One of the few English noble families to survive the conquest and centuries of Norman rule was the Spencer family of Althorp, Lady Diana being the most famous of all.

The Normans are now gone, Normandy is now a province in France. Our Norman Lords all but assimilated, out wed, and out bred. The Norman conquerors have become so much a part of our history and integrated most people see all these place names, castles, fantastically built Christian places of worship Such as Abbeys, Cathedrals and say "I am proud to be English" when really, we all should give a cheeky nod and wink to Hugh and William from Normandy!

19

A Peppered Gaze.

Unveiling the origins of grey eyes through the Barbary pirate trade.

Across the middle east and Northern Africa, many of the beautiful women throughout the region's history have been known to have slate grey or emerald, green eyes. Given the generally accepted genetic make-up of the peoples of these areas it does make you wonder where this trait came from, and quite surprisingly it comes from the desire of an ancient commodity, black pepper.

Black pepper's popularity spread throughout ancient civilizations, including the Egyptians, Greeks, and Romans. It became a highly sought-after spice in the ancient world and was prized for its flavour and medicinal properties. Pepper trade routes, known as the "Pepper Routes," connected to its origins in India to the Middle East, and from there, it made its way to Europe. This is where our story unfolds.

The early trading ships of pepper into Europe were happy to take back their gold, silver, tin, and lead. Pepper was worth a hundred-fold its weight in precious metals and European royal courts would pay anything for it. There are more spices in one single packet of today's tangy cheese Dorito crisps than a medieval peasant family would have consumed in their entire lifetime. That puts the scarcity of exotic spices into perspective and shows pepper (along with other spices) it to be as rare and as fine as frog hair.

The trading ships over a period started to fall under the spell of greed, many not only were traders, but they also became pirates and slavers. They would sail their ships to the coasts of India and load their holds with the precious black peppercorns and other spices, sail their way around to European coastlines selling the spices, once their ships were empty of the pepper they would turn to a more dark and equally as prosperous trade.

The raids began around Scandinavia, Scotland and soon Ireland, then Cornwall became prime targets for a particular type of slave. Gingers, female gingers to be even more exacting. Across the middle east and in some Indian principalities red headed females were like pepper, as in worth more than their weight in gold. Any female child or woman of breeding age or future breeding age was dragged from the coastline villages and taken away by force into lives of slavery for simply being regarded as "exotic".

The pirates carried out these raids for several centuries in ships known as Corsairs, taking many thousands of these women. The trade in slaves was so profitable and normal in the Mediterranean Sea area alone that there were millions of European slaves taken over several centuries, taken from sailing ships attacked by what later became known as "The Pirates of the Barbery Coast". The pirates took their name from the Berber peoples who in antiquity had settled in countrys we know today as Libya, Tunisia, Algeria, and Morocco.

The situation in the Mediterranean became so bad with regard ships being boarded, cargos stolen, and people being sold as slaves that the European countrys banded together and started to fight back. In the 18th century America officially declared war on the Barbary Pirates and there were several full-blown wars against the Barbary Pirates. The trade dissipated as colonial Europe was born and the power of the Ottoman Empire declined.

The sheer volume of European slaves taken is staggering, a fact often overlooked due to it being such a common practice in the middle east that it was not documented like the terrible trans-Atlantic trade. However, the real measure of just how many were taken can be seen in the eyes of modern-day peoples in that area!

20

Horses for Courses.

1000's of years of human life with horses has given us a plethora of adventures together, our city was virtually built with horsepower in its early forms. The area we know as Infirmary Square near the main hospital was known as "The Horse Pool". The rich of the town did not all keep their horses at their homes, their carriages would be housed in their two storey coach houses at the back of their fine city residence and the horses would be sent off to the horse pool for stabling. When a horse or team was required a beggar boy would be given a farthing to go to the horse pool with a message to bring up the said masters horse or horses.

To think of horses, you may generally think of black beauty in a fabulous field setting or maybe historically you may think of a cavalry regiment with all their finery glittering in the sun. I certainly do, three of my relatives were cavalrymen at Waterloo in the 1st Kings Dragoons. Perhaps you saw War

Horse and have a broken heart from those poor creatures in WWI to name but one conflict. Whatever your thoughts on horses; or as my grandparents liked to say "hosses" we can all agree they are majestic creatures and one of nature's beauties.

They seem to have been working for mankind for as far back as the bronze age locally, in Leicestershire out at Glenfield, large amounts of horse related equipment (modern day known as tack) have been found, 2000 years ago horsepower was being harnessed by Leicestershire peoples of the bronze age! The best of the finds were made in the new housing estate behind the hospital area known now as Glenfield Park. The area must have always been regarded as desirable as according to an oral story Gyn the Viking built a great hall in the area for his men to feast in, Gyns Hall modern day said as Gynsills.

I was told a much interesting story about the moving and handling of wagon loads of goods, having only envisaged horses and carts ambling along, perhaps these idealised mental images are inspired by Constables wonderful painting The Haywain and other such wonderful but romantic visions of country life before the camera. (Constables Haywain in the river crossing was "swelling" its wooden wheels in the stream so they were tight in the steel rims that were on the outer edge of the wheels). On an unrelated note, it is hard to believe Constables famous picture was not liked in London upon its grand showing. Thank goodness when it was exhibited in a Paris exhibition, they practically rioted to get to see it and King Charles X of France immediately awarded it a gold medal.

At the top and bottom of many good-sized hills, and esp. hills such as the old Mowmacre Hill up to Thurcaston, or the hill up to the farms on the surrounding hills of present-day Halifax Drive, The Leys of the Earl of Beaumont etc were stables. There would be a stable at the top and the bottom with teams of the largest strongest horses in the county. The waggoners would pay a fee and the great horses would be brought out and added to the waggoners team to haul the heavy loads up the hill. There would also be a fee the tether up the horses to take large loads down the hill with the horses being harnessed at the rear to help the wagons down. The storyteller informed me with great earnest the journey down was by far the most perilous and dangerous job.

Incidentally one of our most well know farms was the Abbey owned "Stockinge Farm". Where farms from around the countryside would bring their animals and goods to be "stocked up" before going onwards into the city! The fees paid to get up that hill must have been most lucrative indeed.

The coming age of steam in the early Victorian era would put many of the working horses out to pasture, the military horses were still in use around the world as late as the 1940's, the Blitzkrieg of the Germans was still powered in the rear by hundreds of thousands of horses and indeed Russian Cossacks on horseback with swords drawn charged German tanks during the invasion of Russia in 1941.

With the utmost respect, I think I prefer my mental image of horse drawn wagons rolling through shaded lanes rather than to war stories.

God bless our four-legged equine friends!

21
It Guzunder the Bed!

Ok, even by my standards this is a strange topic, but it does, it guzunder the bed and if you don't have one that guzunder the bed you can't have your bread, perhaps the nine o'clock horses took you because you didn't go to bed early enough, meaning you did not use your guzunder. If you are of a certain age this will all make perfect sense, if not you are blinking and wanting explanations.

So, the guzunder is a pot bowl, they used to "go under the bed" for weeing in during the night and with Leicester's rich accent it became "the guzunder". The more money you had the nicer the bowl or "potty" was that you had. No-one is ever allowed to do anything serious in the guzunder on pain of death, just a wee. In those days, myself included we were three or four to a bed, top and tailed! (That means you had a pair of feet each side of your face in the bed).

So, there you have it. There is however more to the story, In the era before modern chemicals wee was used by many trades, esp. leather tanners. The leather would be soaked in the unmentionable liquid to soften it to make it workable. So given that almost everything you can imagine was made of leather during and before the Edwardian era you can imagine wee had a value.

In the mornings a fellow would go around the city collecting up the contents of the guzunders and he would pay a few pennies for the pot of much needed liquid. From what I can gather they paid enough for a loaf of bread! So, if you were extremely poor and you did not have a pot you had no bread. This led to the saying "I don't have a pot to pee in" or something similar but rather cruder.

I imagine you are still pondering the nine o'clock horses I mentioned. These were the night soil men. In the city there was no drainage system to take away the more serious matters of human and animal waste. It became necessary for the city leaders to put into place laws as people had been dumping it next to their wells and cholera was rampant.

The job of the night soil man was to traverse the cramped streets of the city after 9pm collecting the bodily waste. It was not a job anyone really wanted, the nightsoil man would be heard coming, the steel rims of the wagon wheels and the steel of the horse's hooves on the granite cobbles echoing through the dark misty coal smoke filled streets. Parents with good reason would pack their children off to bed before "the nine o'clock horses came".

The job of night soil man fell to the people on the fringes of society, it became a job given to many desperate and impoverished agricultural workers displaced by the industrialisation of farming, there are many stories of the nightsoil men taking away stray and orphaned children to the countryside where the nightsoil was used as fertiliser, the orphans often worked on the land for only enough food to keep them working.

As it is close to 9pm and a little misty I think I will end my little story there and go to bed, before I hear the clatter of steel rims and iron clad hooves.

22

The Ghost in the Towers.

In the small, secluded village of Humberstone, nestled between the ancient woodlands and mist-filled dells, was built a foreboding structure that has now loomed over the city for over a century, the infamous county asylum known as "The Towers." Its weathered walls and darkened windows cast an eerie shadow across the area, and the locals whisper chilling tales of the thousands of souls that once inhabited its halls and corridors, just in whispers mind. As the decades have passed the city grew and enveloped the Victorian hospital and its extensive grounds. Saplings planted in the asylums youth now grown high into the skyline, in winter the branches look like hands reaching up and grabbing at the heavens for an escape from this place.

Legend spoke of one particular patient, a man named Cecil, who had been confined to The Towers long ago. Cecil suffered from a mysterious illness that plagued his mind, and the asylum became his eternal home.

Cecil was a huge man, the like of comparing a child's pony to a shire horse. That being said, all who encountered him soon realised he was a gentle lamb with an infectious gentle laugh. He liked to tap people on the shoulder, and when they turned, he would close his eyes and think they could not see him. His tortured soul never did find peace from his demons of his mind, and even after death, he seemed to linger within the asylum's crumbling walls.

For years, locals told tales of those who dared to venture into The Towers and their encounters. Brave souls who worked at the decaying and run down asylum also reported feeling an inexplicable chill in the air, and their breath became visible in the darkness. Some said it was the cold of the afterlife, a reminder of the countless souls who had suffered within these very walls. Others knew exactly and na'ar dare whisper of it for fear of ridicule as they were modern men and women, people educated in science, medicine and only proven facts.

The stories grew more spine-chilling as people claimed to have felt a light tap on their shoulder, as though a long-dead hand reached out from the shadows. Every time they turned to look, there was nothing but darkness and silence. And then, as they turned away, the unmistakable sound of laughter, faint but distinct, echoing through the halls and corridors.

Many believed it was the ghost of Cecil, playing his mischievous game with those who dared to trespass in his domain. Some said he was merely seeking company after spending so many years alone in the darkness of his own mind. Despite the fear and unease, people who encountered Cecil's spirit often spoke after of a strange sense of comfort, as though his presence was not malevolent but rather a reminder of the fragility of life and the bonds that connected the living and the dead, it was the infectious soft laugh of a big but gentle man.

Over time, the asylum closed down, the legend of Cecil and The Towers became woven into the fabric of the town's history. Asylum visits turned into ghostly excursions, with thrill-seekers from far and wide seeking to experience the eerie presence for themselves. The stories persisted in the community, but the ghostly tapping and laughter became folklore as the hospital was reclaimed by nature, great vines growing through the wards and corridors.

As The Towers stories became woven into local legend, so too did Cecil's story. The Towers Hospital was developed and turned into flats and apartments over a decade ago. The new tenants of the dwellings say that even now, when the moon is high, and the mist creeps across the neighbouring fields they feel the occasional tap on their shoulders, and from the dark corners and old recesses they hear a mischievous but gentle laugh from a long gone soul. They turn around and see nothing, except their own breath expelling into the air.

23

The Flesh of Angels for Sale in Leicester.

The books of the bible we know are not the only biblical writings of the time, there are "The Apocrypha" for instance, these contain such things as the book of Tobit, The wisdom of Solomon, The book of Enoch etc. Many believe the priests and clergy of the west do not wish "the great unwashed masses" to know of these books. After reading the book of Enoch for myself I can see why. The Apocrypha and their literary companions from other faiths have given rise to many legends, myths, and fantastical stories. I was told a variation of the story of the angel stones whilst working in the garden and investigated it.

There were four giant mountain sized angels to protect Adam and Eve from the evil serpent who was trying to get them to eat from the tree of knowledge in the Garden of Eden. There was one angel for each of the cardinal directions of the compass, the angel of the north, the angel of the east, the angel of the south and the angel of the west.

The silver-tongued slithering serpent wanted Adam and Eve to eat from the tree of knowledge and then later coerce them to also eat from the tree of life, so they would have all knowledge and live forever. The cunning serpent knew eating fruit from the two trees in the garden of Eden would give mankind great power, but also corrupt them.

The sneaky serpent managed to get Eve to eat the fruit from the tree of knowledge, Eve shared it with Adam and the fall of mankind began. God was very angry with the slithering serpent, but even more so with the angels for failing to protect his newly created children. God only finally forgave womankind upon the birth of Jesus, Jesus's mother Mary is always depicted in statues and paintings with a snake, usually with her feet upon the serpent to show she has crushed its evil and was master of her temptations. Perhaps Adams first wife, Lilith, with her awkward and unyielding nature would have resisted the snake better than Eve who was made to be more subservient than Lilith? We shall never know.

To stop Adam and Eve also eating from the tree of life God banished them from the garden of Eden, Adams punishment was for him and his offspring forever to struggle to produce food. God then set a warrior angel called a cherubim, with a flaming sword to protect Eden until the great flood so mankind could not eat from the lush and bountiful Eden.

God was very angry with the four angels, so he turned them into fire, they burnt so furiously they turned to lava and when cooling they became black stone called obsidian. God struck the four black stone angels with bolts of lightening from the heavens and shattered them into millions of pieces, he then cast the stones to all four corners of, and throughout the earth.

Throughout the history of man, he has coveted the stone obsidian, early cultures created sacrificial blades of obsidian, polished statues of all kinds of pagan gods were made, jewelry of every kind imaginable was forged and mystics polished slabs of obsidian and claimed to see spirits in the reflections.

In many science labs obsidian blades are still used for experiments as they are regarded as the best cutting blades that can be made.

All this aside, nestled in Leicester's old Silver Street is a little shop specializing in selling all manner of curios, crystals, and polished stones, I had a chat with the purveyor of the stones which she said have magical or healing properties. The lady of this little emporium told me that obsidian stones and jewelry are their most popular by a country mile, once picked up they feel compelled to buy she told me with a knowing twinkle in her eyes. I wonder how many people realize they are walking round wearing a necklace or ring made from the essence of an angel from the beginning of our human journey? I know the irresistible piece I picked up in the emporium is nestled in my pocket now.

24
What a Load of Rhubarb!

The red stalks of the rhubarb have a truly alien look, but also a great appeal about them to eager, hungry, and oft greedy eyes of children. I make no excuses for this story not being exactly local; I love rhubarb myself. Hence, I was most intrigued when I heard the term "rhubarb triangle in the garden, of course the yarns started to flow.

Investigations were required to see if any space craft or such had landed in this "Rhubarb Triangle" or had ships and aeroplanes disappeared from radar? No such things, but one story by a very well-known former sports star who claimed to be the son of God (that's a clue to the validity) said "an alien reptilian race was replacing all the powerful humans on the planet, including the Royal family, living in human looking disguises, and living on a diet of rhubarb", and I thought I had imagination.

Firstly, a bit about the plants name. The plant seems to have originated out of far eastern China and is written about in 2700bc, it was known to have grown in pre antiquity in the Himalayas and Mongolia. In some parts of Persia, it was believed the first man and woman were born in a rhubarb plant, Mashya and Mashyanog. It came into eastern Europe around the Volga River 3000 years ago into what we now call Ukraine. The people of the area were called "The Rha" and the Roman word for foreigner is barbarum, put the two together and you have rhubarb, the Romans loved this strange foreign plant and seem to have given it the name we know.

It is thought that the reason rhubarb was only used for medicinal purposes for so long was the leaves are extremely bad for humans. The leaf of the plant has various effects on different people, but they are not good, they damage the kidneys and cause all manner of other discomforts. Do not eat the leaves.

The plant in England really comes into its own in the 1700's, once people realised the stems were good to eat it fast earned the nickname of "The Pie Plant", let's face it, the English can make a pie out of anything, it gained popularity so fast it was soon taken to the "The New World" with the early settlers.

English gardeners set to work on the rhubarb as English gardeners do. It grew best in the north of England, due to the nature of the soil around Yorkshire, with night soil and mill waste thrown onto the fields. The three points of the original vast rhubarb triangle were Leeds, Bradford, and Wakefield.

At first the crop was grown in the fields, however, somehow, it was discovered that growing rhubarb in darkened sheds with a tiny flicker of light created a botanical sprint towards the light, champagne rhubarb was born. It must have looked odd, flickering candles all through the night harvesting, The wonderful things about the rhubarb growing in these conditions were the speed of growth, there are actual recordings of the rhubarb creaking, popping and making low screeching sounds as it grew so very fast. Secondly the rhubarb was sweeter, the plant produced less bitterness. The sheds went up as fast as humanly possible and overnight the rhubarb triangle became an international exporter to vast quantities of the delicious stems. All tended night and day by candlelight even to this day.

The human rhubarb addiction was born, by the time the railways appeared a special railway line was commissioned into the heart of the rhubarb triangle, and in darkened sheds, by candlelight the rhubarb was harvested. At its height two hundred tons of rhubarb was loaded into trains each day and was on the tables of London, Paris, and Rome within a few days. In Ireland a variety was grown that was well over five feet tall, huge leaves and stems as thick as a man's arms.

The rhubarb triangle has shrunk since its days as a giant in the food export market, it is now a triangle formed in Wakefield, Morley and Rothwell, about nine packed square miles of rhubarb. It has achieved a world food heritage site status and only those grown in this area can use the title "Yorkshire Forced Rhubarb" in much the same way cheeses, butters and wines are protected.

Rhubarb is starting to have a resurgence as a recognised superfood, rhubarb is loaded with health benefits, low calorie content has been spotted by dieters. The very dedicated slimmer's have also worked out it speeds up the metabolism. High levels of calcium also mean it is a fat-free alternative to dairy products and it lowers bad cholesterol levels.

This lovely, tart and alien looking plant is definitely back on its way up, we just have to make sure it does not get abducted by reptilian aliens emerging from the strange flickering lights in The Rhubarb Triangle.

25

Coming Home to Roost.

I am not sure if I encounter a particular type of person, but I sure have a lot of poultry, chicken, and all kinds of egg/feather related stories, perhaps it is because we all take them for granted so much? The chicken and egg stories often seem to come about when I inform people that the area where the present-day Leicester Royal Infirmary stands on what was for many years known as "Cock Muck Hill". There was a vast holding area with all manner of sheds and enclosures there for poultry brought in from the countryside for the city to eat. Chickens produce a lot of muck, hence the name for the area.

Chickens and their eggs, simple enough, tasty enough and cheap enough, but where would we be without the humble chicken and egg, even though the chicken did come before the egg.... but that argument is for another story. The humble boiled egg is nature's most perfect packed lunch, it has all you need in the right amounts. When it comes to eggs you might do well to remember you come from an egg, not an egg made in your mother. The egg you came from was made in your grandmother and given to your mother by her before she was born. Human females are born with every single reproductive egg they will ever have, mind blowing, so be sure to thank your maternal granny over tea on Sunday for the egg.

If chickens having better eyesight than humans is hard for you to believe (including the ability to see in ultra violet) I am not sure how you will cope to know they have ears. Those chickens' ears also have a peculiar connection to the colour of the egg that chicken lays. As a rule, if a chicken with white ears lays an egg, the eggshell will be white, if the chicken has brown ears the eggshell will be brown. The cream legbar chicken has blue or green ears, and yes of course, its eggs have corresponding shells. This is not to say nasty mass-produced eggs buck this generalisation.

These chickens with the ears you did not know they had, those ears have different jobs, when another chicken is trying to communicate with it it will tilt its head to listen with its left ear as that seems to be its "chicken speak ear". Their hearing is so good when they sense danger or hear a sound they do not recognise, they turn the head to one side and measure the miniscule amount of different time it takes for the sound to reach each of their ears and from that can measure how far away the possible predator is. This is how good you must be as the most common prey on the planet. Those ears, unlike human ears, also regenerate, chickens and amphibians have perfect hearing until they get old and die (or get eaten).

I could wax lyrical about the use of feathers in human history, you can only make a first-class quill from the big five feathers of the wing of a goose or swan (swan is one of the oldest words in the English language). There was for a while a feather tax on geese, if you ate one you had to pay a tax! This was to fledge arrows for the army, these arrows carried a new kind of tip, the armour piercing bodkin which killed so many French knights at Agincourt. Feathers have always been used, the industrial scale of their use in the industrial revolution became known as "The Ploom boom" and unfortunately wiped-out millions upon millions of birds including several species.

Those rare hens' teeth people talk about, chicks have an egg tooth that they use to break out of the shell, however that falls off after about 24 hours from hatching. You don't really want chickens having teeth to be honest. A long ago very distant relative of the chicken is the pterodactyl, chickens are evolved from dinosaurs, do you really want that kind of thing flying around again, A giant flying chicken with perfect hearing, fantastic eyesight, and a set of teeth like shark? I prefer the one we have, fat, roasted, stuffed with sage and toothless.

26
The Tree of Tears.

A personal story of mine, and an enchanting one for you I hope, takes me back to the late 1970's. During the summers I stayed at my grand-parents little white Aqueduct cottage at the bottom of Zion Hill near Coalville, the tiny Hamlet of Gelsmoor was a place I was transported too often. As tiny as it was, it filled my mind with memories enough for a lifetime. The smoke-filled bustling city where I lived on the Wharf St area was a world away from the little thatched cottage nestled next to the overgrown railway embankment. The thick ancient walls of the cottage, its sparse amenities and its seclusion never subdued the excitement and happiness a stay would bring.

Uncle Sid lived in the next village, Griffydam, my Grandad and I would amble the fields from time to time for a visit and a whisky, yes, I did have a sip or two as a "tasting", (I am sure they gave it to see my facial expressions as I tried to pretend that I liked this at the time, gross drink). It was an adventure filled journey for a young boy with lots to see, rabbits, birds, and all manner of mushrooms, plants, roots, and bushes of which grandad would often grab a part of for salad and for later in the day, of course there were many tastings en route.

One particularly warm day, we were lazily meandering our way up to Griffydam through the fields, me with no shirt on displaying a full set of skinny ribs and sporting a mop of shocking golden hair, grandad sporting his second-best flat cap and his old suit. He always wore his old suit for sweaty "doings", such as gardening, walking, or chopping wood and the likes. I distinctly remember I was playing at being a red coat at Rorkes Drift, I was firing my stick rifle at imaginary Zulu warriors in the bushes with cries of "Zulu to the east Grandad, thousands of them". I would be called a "silly beggar" and next we would be under attack from The Mahadi Army, and I would be Pasha Gordon, oh my poor ole Grandad suffered attacks from foes from every part of the old British Empire as they emerged from my imagination!

One trip we came to pass by a tree we had passed a hundred times amore, but this time it was dripping water from every single extremity, the tips of the branches glistened in the sun as though they had diamond tips. Every tip of every twig and branch end was dripping as fast as a tap, one more drip faster and it would have been a stream. Even at such a young age it was a strange sight to behold, the rays of the sun on the soon to fall droplets twinkled like stars. I truly wish I was a man of great education which is required to describe its magical and enchanting appearance.

I was in and out of the drips, I tasted the splashes on me, they tasted of nothing other than water. As I darted in and out it was like running in and out of the rain, I remember it as clear as yesterday, I can feel the cool spots hitting my skin if I think hard enough. The tree had lost every single leaf even though it was summer, and I enquired to my Grandad what was happening as even at my young age I knew it was unusual.

Grandad was a country man, born and bred of generations of country people, he was in tune and part of the natural order of things. His answer for me was taken as good and true as God's word. For a quiet (unless he had had a few) former miner and simple living man of few words, speaking with his Coalville accent he pulled out a beautiful and most memorable explanation.

"The tree was crying tears of the earth, each tear carries either a good or bad omen, or a slice of good or bad luck, each tear is of sorrow or of joy to come or have been, we will see what happens". I enquired "but there are thousands of drips?" to which the response was "There are millions of people and some of them will never get to feel anything!" Answer accepted without question and onwards I marched, shooting Zulus, Germans and even the Mahdi which ensured Gordon of Khartoum was rescued and didn't die! Off to Uncle Sid's house we went.

The summer passed and I returned to our terraced house on Clyde St, very brown, very blonde and with a large collection of new rifles (sticks), magical stones, jars of pickles and the like. Also, a collection of tales for my jealous city living friends of going to the bingo at Margaret St Club, fizzy pop, lots of sips of beer, crisps with a little blue bag of salt in them and extremely wild rides back to the cottage through winding roads with Uncle Sid, Grandma and Grandad singing loudly in the rusty old mini-van. I realise now everyone was beyond inebriation and approaching oblivion, but what treasured memories for a little boy, they were the last with Grandma as she passed away shortly after, it seems my omen was a sad one this time and it reinforced the story of the tree of tears for me.

Many years have passed now since those days, the people are all physically gone except myself, even though they are very much alive in my heart. I do think back to those days often as my job and interests regularly take me to those areas which are largely unchanged. I now proudly work as a medication delivery driver for The National Health Service (a mobile porter).

One summers day in 2021 as I was walking to one of my tasks, I saw a crowd of people at the Glenfield Hospital taking pictures and gathered around a tree at the back of a building called Mansion House.

They were taking pictures, making videos, and moving about strangely. When I got to them, I realised I had seen this before, there was a tree, it was dripping from every tip and end of branch or twig, my memories were triggered. I joined in, also trying to take pictures and videos of the leafless tree. The pictures did not show much, wet on the ground and a damp looking tree, anyone looking after the fact would have no idea what was witnessed. I told a couple of people present I had seen it afore, all were mesmerised.

I was thrilled to see this occurrence and saw it weeping continually for over a fortnight, oft with a small crowd. I passed the tree several times a day at the time. I started to wonder about the omen for me, after my last experience of a little boy it played a tune of worry to dance in the back of my mind.

A few weeks after the event my omen came to roost. One of the children in the family, whom I had met on a few occasions but had little interaction with, asked something of me. A beautifully special child, she wouldn't leave the house much and who was not very communicative with the world due to autism and appalling experience in the education system, she asked me to take her to the hairdressers. This was a huge deal; she had not had her hair cut for several years by a professional and would physically fight to the death (death usually of the scissor holder) any attempt at the merest trim except by her mother. Her hair was so long she could sit on it with ease. We thought it was due to her quirkiness or autism or a combination. But it was generally thought she just didn't like it cut.

So off we went to the barbers, she didn't want to go to a girl's hairdressers, as a guy I also noticed she had it done in two very thick rope thick pigtails that looked like you could tie one end to a horse and the other to a barge and pull 120 tons of coal along the canal! In we went and off they came, her hair cut ended and it looked like she had joined the marines. High and tight they call it in the forces.

Then came the moment I realised I was being gifted good fortune from the tree of tears, that sentinel of luck, chance and fortunes had blessed me with a child pure of heart, because those rope thick pigtails were picked up by her, then put into my hands with the words "I grew these for the little girls with cancer who lose their hair and I know I can trust you to get it to them to make them happy again".

All those haircuts fought off and now we finally knew why. What a beautiful child with a pure heart has been gifted into my life, compassion is my favourite quality in a person and her veins ran fluid with it and her heart is still to this day crowned with it. From that day to this we have woven a tapestry of tales between us on many adventures and she has grown into a fine young woman with a pure and loving heart to all. As she has grown older, she has become a valued friend as well as my great niece.

To the tree itself, as I am older and hopefully wiser, I investigated the one at Glenfield hospital and I investigated high and low, far, and wide. It is a simple sycamore tree, about 25-30 years old. I could find no references to this phenomenon locally, and no similar stories amongst the encyclopaedically knowledge knowing volunteer gardeners in The Secret Garden at Glenfield hospital. If this collection of brilliant botanically minded folks didn't know I did begin to doubt myself.

Fate decided to give me a hand, as I was path washing in the garden a fellow started to make conversation with me, he had been to have his heart scanned. After some chitchat I enquired what he did, he was an arborist at a university in London. So, we chatted about the trees close by and then I asked him about the tree that cried.

He was quite excitable, smiley, and said he had never seen one and I was extremely lucky to have seen it as it was a very rare occurrence, but he knew of the phenomena. it was a tree protecting itself from petrifying ground water. At first, I thought he had been reading to many Harry Potter books, however, he elaborated. There is a type of water that can slowly turn things into stone due to its chemical makeup. If a tree's water supply becomes contaminated by this water the tree will drop its leaves and flush itself through its branch tips for as long as it is able; to be rid of the bad water to save itself. Many trees die as they are unable to outlast the volume of bad water before they turn to stone, but some, like the one at Glenfield, survive it by washing through the bad petrifying water until its replaced by clean untainted water.

I have investigated this in some very old archives, there is a petrifying spring listed on a 15th century survey at lower Griffydam, there is also a petrifying well listed in Glenfield, Woodcocks well. I have looked for the well at Glenfield but have yet to locate it, but the Zion Hill Griffydam spring is still there and approximately in the right place.

Across the world there are all manner of trees crying tears in folklore from almost every culture, Aboriginal, Cherokee, Korean, Filipino, Welsh, and Japanese to name but a few places. All have the same things in common, its rare, its ancient and it carries an omen.

About half a century has passed since my encounter with the tree of tears between Griffydam and Zion Hill. The tree of tears at Glenfield Hospital only three years ago at time of scribing this. It is nice to know we share with our own ancestors, all kinds of tribes and peoples around the world, The Trees of Tears. I hope you see a good teardrop in your life's journey.

Tree artwork by Jevgenija Zulfugarova.

27
The Giants of Belgrave.

There is an old folk story about how Belgrave in Leicester got its name, I first heard the story from my niece, Stacey Louise Goodwin of Mowmacre Hill. It surprised me that I did not know the story as I am 20 years her senior, a know it all; and what's known as "A Belgrave boy". My father and his father before him were also Belgrave boys (Jeff Goodwin and Eric Goodwin res), as well as my grandmothers Billington side all living in Belgrave from the time before records began. Here is what Stacey Louise taught me: -

Many years ago, when
giants roamed the land a boastful
giant called Bell said he could get to
Leicester in three mighty leaps.
To prove this, he mounted his sorrel mare
at a place called Mountsorrel and took
his first mighty leap.

He jumped over Rothley and landed in Wanlip (one leap).

He then jumped a second time and
landed in Birstall, so called because
his horse "burst its all" and couldn't go on.
His third and final leap landed
one and a half miles short of
Leicester and there he died from the effort and was buried
in a place called Belgrave (Bell's Grave).

So that's the story of one ancient giant, but you know there is another & not all of Belgrave's giants are ancient. I want to tell you about a giant that every old Belgrave child had known personally for at the very least one hundred & fifty years. This giant is still alive, but only just, it's in the last ebbs of its long life, measured at a point of over 2 metres above the ground the tree is over four metres round. This makes the giant tree over two hundred & thirty years old, it has a botanical name, Aesculus Hippocastanum. To the kids of Bath Street, it was "The Conker Tree". If you said to your mates "I'll meet you at the conker tree" you did not need to ask which one, it was so majestic.

I would think the climbing would have really started when it was about 70. The tree sits on the slight incline from the lower children's park, Belgrave Meadow up into Belgrave Gardens Park, everyone I know calls it "Talbot Park", as for the tree; it dominated the skyline all my adult life.

Climbing this tree was a rite of passage for most of Belgrave's children, apart from collecting the conkers for stringing; the male children of Belgrave were expected to climb this giant, I myself climbed it, I would estimate the main climb was 120-150 feet. I climbed it to the top for my first time with my mates, Mickey Coughlin and Dave "Moggy" Morrison, part of The Bath Street Gang as we called ourselves, there were many of us, it was in the days when "gang" meant a group of kids adventuring together.

The view was incredible, from the top of this leafy giant, you could see all across the city, all the now gone factories with their smoking chimneys towards the city and the other way, out towards Bradgate, on most days you could clearly see Old John Hill with Stamford's Folly atop looking like its well-known beer mug shape. (yes, old John is the name of the Hill, the beer mug tower is actually Stamford's Folly).

I have not been to Talbot Park for a few years, I live at Rushey Mead now, so I decided to take my dog for a walk whilst off from work one day. As I walked from Belgrave Hall I noticed right away as soon as I walked in the park that the great giant was standing wounded, almost slain. I took a deep sigh and made towards the scene. I never thought a tree would induce such trepidation...

I rounded the bend and there it stood, butchered and bloodied:-

I understood the tree was dying, I could see its hollowed-out heart, it was being eaten alive from the inside. This still did not stop the feeling of great sorrow for the loss of this Belgrave giant, one who carried the children of the area on its shoulders for generations. I remember the days when this giant had perhaps 20 children in it chattering like a flock of birds.

There will be no headstone for this giant, no village named after it like boasting Bell, and it has no known name other than "The Conker Tree". But what there are is hundreds if not thousands of adults, who whence children knew it and who have memories of swinging from its branch's and collecting and stringing its seeds for a playground game. I hope this little story stirs those memories and that the dying giant can rest easy, its job to the youth and childhood of mankind well done.

28

Leicestershire's Other Lost King.

In the heart of Leicestershire's rich historical tapestry, where a king has found his resting place in a car park, another crowned in our shire at Stoke Golding and Queens like Jane Grey left their mark, the tale of a Gypsy King, Absalom Smith, unfolded with an air of importance rivalling the grandest royal narratives, however he has never received the recognition he deserves befitting a king.

Perhaps it is because he died as the industrial revolution was really starting to steamroll, the year was 1826, the British Empire was awash with news and history making events, so it is time to cement his reign into our local history properly, So I beg you to indulge in my yarn.

The Gypsies, some whispered, were descendants of pharaohs, their name stemming from an ancient translation of Egyptians, I can see it, "E-gypsy ians". Others believed their dark complexions were a result of the dispersing of Alexander the Great's army in the Punjab region of northern India, where they married the daughters of Kings, Maharajas, and Princes. From these ancient roots, the Gypsies wandered across Europe, evolving into the diverse groups we know today.

Absalom, the Gypsy King, was a man of opulence derived from the streams surrounding the village of Twyford in Leicestershire, gold pulling was a local source of income. The village itself owed its name to the dual forded streams, Twyford, twice forded.

Absalom's reputation as a virtuoso fiddler drew admirers from far and wide, captivating audiences at the Saddle pub and every significant event in the village, from births, marriages to wakes. It was said he could fiddle so well he could call up a storm.

It was during one such performance at The Saddle Inn that Absalom's fate took a malevolent turn. He became stricken by illness; he was transported to the royal gypsy camp at Friesland on a nearby lane. Dr Noble, the most esteemed physician in the shire was summoned from Dannetts Hall and he attended to him at an astronomical cost of 5 Guineas per visit. Rumours circulated that Absalom's musical prowess had roused the envy of Lucifer himself, prompting the devil to cast a fatal spell upon the gifted fiddler, the Christian Dr Noble would have none of it.

Absalom, a figure of immense stature, succumbed to his mysterious ailment in early February of 1826. The Gypsy tribe gathered to bid their king farewell with a ritualistic pyre, a blaze that consumed all of Absalom's possessions, it was their way to gift a good afterlife. He left thirteen children and 124 grandchildren, they, along with members from twelve other tribes watched in their multitudes as Absalom's caravan and chattels went up in flames.

One of his daughters was a noted stunning beauty named Beatta, who would capture the lord's gaze, she also watched as the caravan went up in flames. Beatta's portrait, draped in a fine red robe, found its place in Belvoir Castle, a testament to her captivating allure. She alone was noted for having 24 children.

Yet, amidst the consuming fire, one item remained untouched—the fiddle that had enchanted countless souls. Absalom, in his royal blue coat adorned with silver buttons, was laid to rest in a grave rumoured to be 12 feet deep. Layers of clay, oak slats, and stones shielded his grave goods, preserving the secrets of his afterlife.

The mystery deepened around King Absalom as the fiddle had defied the fiery fate of all its owner's other possessions. In the misty lanes around Twyford, those who listen carefully often swear they hear the haunting strains of a fiddle. A tune so well played, it resonated through the fields and hedgerows like the voice of an angel, a sweet sound befitting a king's ears. Some believed it to be Absalom's spirit, the echoes of his enchanted fiddle singing a ghostly story through the centuries.

The legend lives on, and the ethereal music lingers, reminding all who hear it that Absalom Smith, the Gypsy King, is not forgotten.

29

A Towering Tale.

Looking down London Road from the gates of Victoria Park is a very interesting view, many of the landmarks you know so well can be seen. Top Hat Terrace, Blunts, The Free Masons Hall, Peat Tower, and much more, it is a visual feast. In this picture by the amazing Leicester photographer, Mat Fascione the view is from University Road (he kindly gave permission to use the images in this article). You will agree and are probably nodding your head in agreement when I say Leicester folk know this view well.

However, you might have missed something, look again and you will see a massive volcano in the background, looming over the city! You can discuss that one with other Leicester folks and wonder how you missed it all those times you were there.

The amazing scene in the far background is of course Bradgate Park, gifted to the city by Charles Bennion. The history of the park and the nine-day Queen Jane Grey are all very well-known stories.

One of the most prominent symbols used for our city and shire is the beer mug shaped tower high on one of the hills of Bradgate. Old John is the name springing into the back of your mind. I'll tell you a little-known story about the most famous tower in our shire.

William Rider and Thomas Henfry were good friends, they set off to Nottingham from Barrow upon Soar just after Christmas early in 1784. Both the men were farm workers, William was noticeable as he was a huge and powerful man. As their journey went, they worked along the way, by February they were working in Peascroft Field at Bingham, being paid in beer and food.

William and Thomas got far too drunk one cold February day whence they came across the well to do James Caunt meandering along on his nag at the bottom of Bingham Hill. For a reason lost in time they decided to rob him, and they took all he had, 5 golden guineas, some silver, some copper coins, and some small gemstones/trinkets of very high value. They committed highway robbery and were now wanted highwaymen!

It was not long before the two were in a tavern spending their booty, the building was soon surrounded by the local Yeomanry. When they realised they were surrounded William decided to swallow some of the gems and trinkets, thinking he might escape and retrieve them later. The two highwaymen surrendered and were taken off to Nottingham Castle for trial.

After quickly being found guilty and sentenced to hang they were taken out of the castle on the back of a cart, William throwing off his shoes and shirt for the watching crowd with the cry of "I won't need these where I am going".

On 31st March 1784 Thomas Henfry was strangled by the hangman's rope as the cart moved away from under his feet. William saw this grotesque death and decided he would make his death quicker.

The rope was placed around William's neck and just before the cart was moved, he jumped over the side of the cart as high in the air as he could, expecting to break his neck and attain a quick, clean death rather than the wriggling strangling he had just witnessed bestowed upon his friend.

A macabre scene unfolded, William was a huge man, his weight caused his head to come clean off and roll to the feet of the watching crowd, women fainted, and children cried out. The scene became even more horrific, Williams body landed on its feet and balanced for a few moments as if standing headless and undead but not alive.

More gasps and shrieks followed as his body dropped to his knees, paused in balance again and as the now silent mob watched it fell forward, his offal's and innards spewing out his neck, and in these offal's and innards twinkled the jewels and gemstones.

The crowed surged forward and grabbed in the mess shamelessly. In the crowd was a well-known figure, Mr William Wilberforce the slavery abolitionist who was on his way to Yorkshire on parliamentary business. He ordered the Yeomanry to gain control of the scene. He also ordered that Williams head be salted and sewn into a pigskin bag and sent to Leicester Castle for inspection by the surgeons to see if they could find out what had sent him “evil of ways”. At the time surgeons were only allowed to “open up” the dead if they were criminals, they would think Williams head a great prize.

Mr Wilberforce had also just retained two Nottingham stone masons and their apprentices for the employ of Thomas Sketchley of Leicester who was contracted to build a tower for his Wilberforce’s friend, The Earl of Stamford.

So, off the masons went, two shillings a piece to deliver the salted head in a pigskin bag to Leicester Castle and then onwards to build the tower at Bradgate.

The tower the masons with the grizzly tale built has a proper name, The Earl of Stamford’s Folly, or “Stamford’s Folly”. The Earl liked to watch his horses race around the base of the hill, that’s why he had the folly built from the remains of the old windmill on Old John Hill.

Old John Folly, Bradgate Country Park, Leicestershire

So, I present to you a fine picture of the correctly named Stamford's Folly in the full knowledge you will still forever call it "Old John", but at least you know the story of William Rider, the headless Highwayman of Barrow upon Soar!

Wonderful pictures by local photographer Mat Fascione ©

30

All's Well That Ends Well.

About halfway up London Road heading out past the Mayfield Island are Springfield Road, adjacent is Clarendon Park Road. The land between these new roads was originally an open space of farmland as was most of the land either side of the then gravel London Road. There was even a turnstile and toll house at each end! It was mainly developed during the Victorian era, many of the fine houses on London Road were built by "toffs" who could no longer afford to keep huge country mansions due to changes in land tax and death duty taxes. The closures and changes towards the end of this social change are very well portrayed in the excellent tv series Downton Abbey.

During construction on some of the upper middle-class houses of Springfield Road and Clarendon Park Road there were problems with wet soggy ground, the clue being in the original name of the farmland "The Spring Field". It was a rather troublesome spring; Springfield Road was to be an apt name indeed.

When the attempts to stem the spring subsided the Victorians flourished as they did with many such challenges. Their ingenuity led to the spring being piped into a large natural artisan well which is underneath the Highfields area. The genius is just beginning.

The new influx of regular water flowed out the Highfields artisan well naturally using hydrostatic equilibrium, which is an ancient pump-free technique, into "the New Leicester Water Conduit", which ran into the centre of the city along Upper and Lower Conduit Street. Conduit Street is still there today at the side of the train station.

The conduit fed a very large well at the Leicester city centre, known as "The Central Grand Well, it is in the centre of the small St Martins shopping area and I believe still has a large and decorated lid upon it. This well had overflow pipes which topped up wells all over the city centre, which, in those days, was up near Jubilee Square.

The central well topped up wells out as far as Wharf St, Humberstone Road, and St Margarets Church.

It was indeed further used to somehow provide pressure to water the vegetable gardens of St Margaret's Church and vicarage, where Burleys Way, Crafton Place, Crane Street, and the bus station are today all this from the troublesome spring up London Road.

I remember the story of the overflows going this far, as due to leaks around St Margarets church, the bodies under the floors of the church were supposedly and according to my grandad, a builder called Eric Goodwin to have been "floating out of their rotting coffins, banging on the underside of the floorboards under the pews" he elaborated "they then knew the overflow pipes needed rodding out".

The information regarding the well system was given to me by my father, Jeff Goodwin, an old Leicester builder and the information is corroborated by my father-in-law, Fred Parrott, who covered over and/or repaired many such wells in the basements of the big department stores with steel plates, whilst working for well-known J C Kellett and Sons.

The knowledge builders pass to their apprentice sons is more than just how to lay bricks! The last time I worked on a well in Leicester was on the back of High Street, just before the Millennium.

It was approximately 100ft deep. The building inspector and council officials upon inspection knew the well and were of the opinion it would first have been a walled well during Roman times.

The top part of the well was Victorian brick. The brickwork underneath was a mismatch of out-of-place Northampton stone and artisan fired bricks, as it went lower it was hard to see what was there as didn't go down.

During my time as a bricklayer, I saw wonders under the streets of Leicester that today, just 20-30 years later, would be treated as archaeological treasure, I often wonder if the spring still fills the wells and wonder more if they ever hear the knocking on the underside of the floors in St Margarets Church!

31

End Blast.

I was born just off Wharf St in 1966 and have prospered since, as I reach an older age, I have realised that at the beginning of life and as you enter the end period you should never trust a fart.

32

A final word from the author.

I have enjoyed writing this book, I do hope it will prompt you to investigate and question what was written, this could lead you into many adventures and will enable you to find and perhaps write your own versions of the stories, or even pass them on verbally. I cannot state enough that there is a lot of embellishment as there always is with the subject matters which I covered, I do hope I at least entertained.

I cannot enough thank the volunteer gardeners of the Secret Garden where I worked and shielded for a year during the covid lockdown. They are brilliantly led by Sue Stevenson, the gardeners themselves are a lovely group. They are based at the back of Mansion House in the grounds of Glenfield Hospital, they gave me much encouragement to write the stories down. I have never met such a selfless collective and truly they have made a difference to not only my life, but to the wellbeing of thousands of patients and visitors to the hospital, in particular those being treated in the Bennion Centre and Bradgate Units where I have heard personal testimony from patients of the contribution the garden has made to their recovery. The gardens worked by the volunteers have actually helped to get much loved sick people back into their homes and the arms of their loving families. I have become one of them and wear the shirt with great pride.

The original artworks in the book have been done by people I like greatly or love. It really mattered to me who contributed greatly. Richard T Paling painted and designed the cover for me, I feel like my book is wrapped in his talent. Other friends of mine did the drawings, Seema, Jen and Pammie all did a wonderful job, my nephew, Josh Fletcher took the picture on the back cover. I also owe a debt of gratitude to Robin Oxley-Boyle for his publishing advice.

There is the matter of my wife to thank, Rachel, who as always has been at my side in this literary endeavour, reading editing and helping. With this wonderful woman I have led the life of which as many as two dozen men or more could not have. We have adventured near, far and wide together, my cup overflows with blessings and love from my marriage, she brings me the peace and council that men such as Kings and Emperors seek.

So, my last words in this book are for me the best words I ever got to say in my life: -

I love you, Rachel.

Derek Charles Goodwin

Derek Charles Goodwin is an amateur local historian with a particular passion for family history. He is a member of the The Leicestershire and Rutland Family History Society as well as several online history groups.

Although short on formal education and traditional literary lessons, his writings are entertaining, endearing and truly worth the investment of your precious time. More books are planned to be released for publication in the near future.

Derek volunteers at The Glenfield Secret Garden to refresh his soul and lift his spirit.

His hobbies include playing chess, collecting commonwealth stamps and enjoying his extensive model railway.

Derek married his beautiful and cultured wife, after which they travelled the world extensively together, then returned and settled down in the suburbs of Leicester.

www.ingramcontent.com/pod-product-compliance
Lightning Source LLC
LaVergne TN
LVHW012059160826
845678LV00014B/2884

* 9 7 8 1 7 3 8 5 5 4 1 1 9 *